Lustful Maidens
and
Ascetic Kings

Lustful Maidens
and
Ascetic Kings

Buddhist and Hindu Stories of Life

Roy C. Amore
Larry D. Shinn
Illustrations by Sharon Wallace

New York   Oxford   Toronto
OXFORD UNIVERSITY PRESS
1981

Copyright © 1981 by Oxford University Press, Inc.

Library of Congress Cataloging in Publication Data
Amore, Roy C   1942-
Lustful maidens and ascetic kings.

Bibliography: p.
1. Tales, Indic.
2. Tales, Indic—History and criticism.
I. Shinn, Larry D., 1942-   joint author.
II. Title.
GR305.A46   398.2'0954   80-19740
ISBN 0-19-502838-4   ISBN 0-19-502839-2 (pbk.)

Printed in the United States of America

This book is dedicated to
Philip Ashby
and
Paul Clasper
two mentors whose love of
Hindu and Buddhist stories
was contagious.

Acknowledgments

Our children, Christie, Allison, Robyn, and Justin, are to be appreciated for their incessant pleas for "just one more story" at bedtime. Their eager anticipation and interspersed comments have made the magic of many Indian stories and storytelling come· alive for their fathers. From the animal fables of the *Panchatantra* and the *Jatakas* to the fantastic tales of the exploits of Rama or a Buddhist monk, our children have shown us new ways to look at old stories. While we found social and religious values in the stories of Hindus and Buddhists, our children found new friends and funny animals, new superheroes and their enemies.

We also acknowledge the encouragement given us by our university students year after year. Their great enthusiasm for stories such as these was matched by the knowledge of India gained thereby.

A special word of appreciation must be expressed to Judy Amore, whose editorial skills and hours of patient work improved the manuscript immensely.

October 1980   L.D.S.
                                                                 R.C.A.

Contents

Lustful Maidens
and
Ascetic Kings

Introduction
Storytelling in India

Long ago in the city of Mahilaropya lived a king who was righteous and wise. He was also generous and treated his subjects fairly while taxing them very lightly. This virtuous king had three slow-witted sons and fretted over his task of teaching them the laws and duties of kingship. He called in his ministers for their counsel and said, "Advisors, you already know that my three sons are complete fools and slow to learn their lessons. I can see little profit in the birth of a son if he be neither virtuous nor wise. What can a man do with a cow which gives neither milk nor calves? Still, it is my duty to provide instruction for my sons in the duties of kingship, and I now ask your advice as to the best means."

One minister responded, "Your majesty, you know that the study of Sanskrit grammar takes twelve years to complete before a student can progress to the study of moral obligations, the art of love, and the means of worldly success. This is a difficult assignment even for the intelligent pupil to accomplish; how much more troublesome for the dull-witted. Still, I have heard that

3

there is a brahman named Vishnusharman who is famous for his wisdom and teaching skill." The king was pleased to hear his minister's report, and summoned Vishnusharman at once.

When the elderly sage was brought and seated before the king, the anxious monarch said, "Noble brahman, I beg you to help me in the education of my three dull sons so that they may be counted as second to none in the knowledge of their princely duties. I will give you a fortune in gold if you are able to accomplish this task." The wise old teacher replied, "Your majesty, since I am old and my senses are numbed by the passage of time, the age for me to enjoy a fortune in gold is past. Still, what you ask me to do is a challenge to my teaching skill and I gladly accept this difficult task. In fact, if by the end of six months I have not raised your sons' knowledge above all their peers, you may banish me from your kingdom as an imposter!"

When the king and his ministers heard the sage's incredible promise, they at once turned the three idiot princes over to him for instruction. The proud and venerable sage then composed the Five Books of Princely Fables (the *Panchatantra*) and by these animal tales achieved his appointed task.

This account of the origin of the *Panchatantra* illustrates the importance Indians place upon storytelling as an instructional device. The many collections of myths (e.g., *Puranas*) serve as vehicles of lay religious education in a culture where literacy is low but storytelling abounds. Animal fables, fairy tales, epic stories of cultural heroes, narratives of the previous lives of the Buddha, and regional folktales of all kinds have been a part of India's oral culture for over three thousand years. These narratives are conveyed by folk-singers, priests, dramatists, and parents in all the Indian dialects. Festivals, daily temple recitations of poetry and scripture, dramas, and songfests all provide occasions for transmission of the tales which instruct, admonish, and simply entertain Indian children as well as adults.

4

To grow up in India is to mature in a world alive with demons and water nymphs, goblins and irate goddesses. Wisdom is often measured not by degrees or formal education, but by the ability to tell the right story or recite a passage of scripture appropriate to a particular situation. Mothers and fathers teach their children religious and family responsibilities through stories. Householders scold their servants with reference to the fate of a character in a particular tale. In classical times, the student priest had to commit to memory vast quantities of scriptures, which varied in subject matter from the techniques of sacrifice to the proper conduct of the king in peacetime and at war. The moral tales and fables as well as myths relating the feats of the gods were common fare for any person who sought to be educated.

Sources

The specific sources for the stories told herein are listed at the end of this work. To place such sources in the history of Indian literature would require a book of equal length to this one, but to note some broad features of Indian story telling and collecting can be instructive. First of all, since stories are transmitted orally in the first instance, the same story may be found in different versions in written sources quite distant from each other in time. For example, the famous story of the god Vishnu assuming a dwarf's form to trick a demon king out of his ill-gotten rule of the universe, is mentioned in the earliest Aryan collection of hymns in Sanskrit called the *Vedas* (c. twelfth century B.C.) and is repeated in various writings down to the *Bhagavata Purana* (c. ninth century A.D.). Secondly, the sharing of stories from one time period to another is mirrored in the use of the same story by different religious traditions in the same era. For example, the story of the donkey disguised in a lion's skin appears in Hindu and Buddhist literature, as well as in Greek fable collections. Thirdly, in spite of the fluid movement of stories through time and traditions, In-

5

dian stories are "frozen" periodically in story collections evidencing a wide variety of purposes and designs.

The earliest Indian literature, the *Vedas*, consists of hymns to various gods, whose stories are more often assumed than told. The dozens of references to various stories, however, have given credence to the primary importance of story in this earliest period of Indian literature and religion. The threads of this early Sanskrit mythological tradition persist throughout later priestly writings, the *Brahmanas* (c. 900 B.C.), and reach full bloom in the "Legends" of the gods, the *Puranas* (c. 300-900 A.D.). Alongside this development of myths and legends, didactic moral fable collections began to emerge (200 B.C.-200 A.D.). One early fable collection was the *Panchatantra* or "Five Wisdom Books" from which several of our stories come. Concurrently, the Buddhists borrowed many of the fables used in other contexts to tell of the many "Previous Births" of the Buddha (the *Jataka* tales of the Pali Canon, the Buddhist scripture dating from the second century B.C.). These narratives form the source for many of the Buddhist tales told in the pages which follow.

The two Indian epics, the *Ramayana* and the *Mahabharata*, have also long been reference points for priest, teacher, or parent in locating instructive stories. The *Mahabharata* is ostensibly a story with a single narrator about the great war of two rival families of cousins who contest each other's right to rule India in the early golden days. In fact, the *Mahabharata* is a collection of several story traditions compiled over four or five centuries (third century B.C. to second century A.D.) which provides advice and instruction for earthly pursuits as well as spiritual advancement. Within the framework of this famous war story literally hundreds of ancillary stories are told. Its most famous section is the *Bhagavad Gita* ("Song to the Lord") which extols the purpose and might of the god Vishnu and the necessity of devotion to him. The *Ramayana* of Valmiki (200 B.C.-200 A.D.), on the other hand, is a shorter story less intermixed with divergent tales, which tells of the life of King Rama and the abduction and release of his beautiful wife Sita. Still, the various recensions of this story reveal the work of many hands. Stories from both of these epic compilations are represented in the tales which follow.

Function

Whether pan-Indian or local, stories have been and continue to be a primary vehicle of religious instruction in India. Reading, reciting, hearing, singing, and remembering the myths of one's chosen god is a basic and required devotional act. Furthermore, those who receive and transmit the holy narratives can expect to achieve worldly success as well as spiritual rewards. Nearly all Indian story collections end with some statement about the efficacy of hearing and telling the stories enclosed. One good example is the comment found at the end of the *Ramayana:* "He who listens to this marvellous story of Rama shall be forgiven all his sins. By listening to the feats of Rama a son, wealth, or a husband will be granted those who desire them. They who read or hear these sacred verses shall obtain all their desires and all their prayers shall be answered." Such is the importance attached to many of the Buddhist and Hindu stories preserved in oral, and now written, form.

From the thousands of stories available we have selected sixty-five that meet the following two criteria:

First, each story has been used for instruction. The stories included in this book provide models for social roles or religious values. In many cases the model behavior is exemplified by the story's main character, but almost as often the main character is an example of immoral or improper behavior, and the reader is encouraged to behave in the opposite way. We will refer to the positive examples as "models for" behavior and the negative examples as "images of" behavior.* For example, the story "Savatri

---

* For a good discussion of this twofold function of religious symbols and stories, see Clifford Geertz, "Religion as a Cultural System," in *Anthropological Approaches to the Study of Religion,* ed. by Michael Banton (London: Tavistock Publications, 1966), pp. 1-46.

and the God of Death" provides a *model for* the ideal wife, whereas "The Carpenter's Wife" furnishes an *image of* the wife as an untrustworthy, lustful creature.

Second, each story is entertaining. Most stories which were morally instructive but not entertaining fell into oblivion centuries ago. What survive in any culture are the stories that the people of that culture love to hear. The endings are satisfying in the sense that the bad people are punished and the good are rewarded. Many of the stories are somewhat larger than life, and they would not be so entertaining if they were not. For example, the story of Sita ("The Test of Fire") provides a model for sexual fidelity in a woman who demonstrates her chastity by emerging from a raging fire unharmed.

Context

The original stories take for granted that the reader is Indian and therefore familiar with Indian rituals, customs, and world view. Since our goal has been to tell the stories in a lively style understandable to readers not familiar with India, we have translated the stories very freely from their Sanskrit and Pali originals. To meet this goal, we have omitted much of the repetition occurring especially in Buddhist stories, abridged and retold lengthy narratives, and occasionally added a word or phrase to make an intended reference or meaning clear to non-Indians. However, there are some themes which recur in many of the stories without being fully explained in any of them, so we wish to comment upon them here. For example, frequently we read that one god, named Indra in the Hindu stories and Sakka in the Buddhist stories, gets a hot throne when a human meditates or performs austerities with great success. The underlying assumption for this image is that practices such as meditation, asceticism, and self-mortification create a mystic heat (*tapas*) which purifies the practitioner. However, when the heat becomes intense because of unusually severe asceticism or unusual virtue, the power of the heat reaches all the way up to the heavenly realm of the gods. This may heat up the whole of the heavens, and all of the gods' residences, but in most of the stories it specifically causes the marble throne of the king of the gods (Indra or Sakka) to become uncomfortably hot. The god always worries about this because he fears that the meritorious human who is causing the heat intends to displace him. It is assumed that the gods themselves gained their high offices by practicing asceticism and virtue, and that they can be replaced by someone who is even more ascetic or virtuous. With this in mind, the gods usually come down to earth to try to disrupt or corrupt the potential usurper.

Another recurring story motif involves the practice of granting a boon. In several stories a master or a god responds to someone's great service by offering to grant him or her a reward for meritorious service. It is expected that the servant will choose a boon of riches or of long life, but many of the characters of the stories make surprising requests for loved ones or for spiritual knowledge.

The reader of these stories should also have in mind the common Indian distinction between "householder" and "monk." A "householder" is the male head of a house, but the term also applies to everyone who lives a non-monastic lay life. That is, householders are all those men and women who have not abandoned the family life for the ascetic path of the religious seeker. The "monks" on the other hand are those who have "departed from the world," that is, from the secular, worldly life. They live under vows of celibacy, poverty, and homelessness. They may live in monasteries, forest hermitages, or parks. Or they may wander, alone or in groups, from place to place. Most who took such vows were men, but the Buddhists and some other Indian religious traditions had monastic orders for women as well.

Finally, several of our tales are taken from collections told around a frame story. For example, all the stories which begin with a goblin posing a riddle-story to a king named Vikram come

9

from the collection of tales entitled "Twenty-five Tales of the Goblin." According to the frame story, King Vikram is tricked by an evil brahman (a member of the priestly class) into carrying a goblin from a cemetery to a goddess's temple. To accomplish his task, the king must maintain silence, yet the goblin continues to pose riddles through stories which entice the king to speak, so the goblin is able to return to his tree in the graveyard. Twenty-four times King Vikram begins his journey anew with the storytelling goblin on his back.

Another frame story lies behind many of the Buddhist stories in this book. According to Buddhist tradition many eons ago a young man vowed some day to become an Enlightened One, a Buddha. From that time on he was known as the Future Buddha (Bodhisattva), and he experienced hundreds of rebirths, that is, lived hundreds of times. The Buddhists collected various stories (fables, moral stories, folktales) under this frame story. In the Pali language collection which we draw upon in this book, there are over five hundred such Birth Stories (*Jatakas*). The Future Buddha's final rebirth, as Gautama the Buddha, provides the material for the stories "Buddha Sets the Wheel in Motion," "Buddha Finds a Middle Path," and "The Dying Buddha's Compassion." The literary device of telling one story as the occasion to tell many other diverse stories is common in the oral traditions of India.

Interpretation

A final word must be said with regard to the interpretation of the following stories as *models for* and *images of* family and religious roles and values. We are quite aware of the variety of approaches and interpretations applied to Indian mythology and folklore. Much is to be gained from structuralists' assertions regarding the bipolarity of Indian mythic thought and expression. Likewise, psychoanalytic attempts to fathom Indian fables and

10

folklore to reveal certain unconscious dimensions of the joint family, the monastic path, or Indian sex roles are valuable. In addition, sociological interpretations and anthropological analyses of Indian stories lay bare much content that is peculiar to Indian social groups or universal among all peoples. Therefore, it is quite clear that the chosen interpretation exposes only one level of influence Indian stories have. *As multilayered vehicles of meaning, Indian stories are not to be fully digested as "models" alone.* Nonetheless, among the many functions stories have and the meanings they convey, none is more apparent than their role as cultural and religious guideposts. Whether young boy or girl, husband or wife, skeptic or priest, images of the errant life and models for proper conduct and living abound in Indian story traditions. And it is that panoramic display from lustful maidens to ascetic kings the reader is now invited to survey.

1
Family Roles

From the ancient clan grouping (*gotra*) to the contemporary joint family, the Indian family has been understood to include not only the parents and children, but also the brothers, sisters, grandparents, and cousins living under one roof. Consequently, blood ties have always been important in determining marriage partners and allies. For example, the heart of Arjuna's concern in the great war between cousin families (as told in the *Mahabharata* epic) was that he, as a warrior, would have to fight the cousins and uncles with whom he grew up (*Bhagavad Gita*, Ch. 1). Thus, the family is a good place to explore the roles that Indian folktales mirror and prescribe.

Buddhist stories reflect the same Indian cultural roles and values seen in the Hindu stories, so far as life within a family ("householder life") is concerned. But Buddhism's emphasis differed radically from that of Hinduism when it encouraged young men to "depart from the world" and take up the life of a celibate monk. We will return to this Buddhist call to asceticism. Here we wish to retell Hindu and Buddhist stories which communicate images and models of family roles.

MAN
Hindu Stories

The roles of husband and father are the keystone of all familial roles. In traditional Indian literature which records the four basic (though admittedly ideal) religious stages of every man's life, the stage of the householder (husband and father) is regarded as the superior one. A classical Hindu ethical code, the *Laws of Manu* (6.87, 89, 90) says, "The student, the householder, the forest-dweller and the ascetic comprise the four stages of life, but all of these stages spring from that of the householder. . . . As all rivers, both large and small, flow into the ocean, so it is that men of all stations of life find protection with householders. . . . Because men of the other three orders are daily supported by the householder, it is the householder's which is the best of all stations."

Only if a man is married is he permitted to perform life-giving sacrifices according to ancient Hindu custom. Likewise, it is only a married man who is charged with the responsibilities of ritually remembering the ancestors, honoring the gods, and providing sons to continue the family line. The value of a man's role in the Indian family is high indeed. In the story which follows, the three roles of father, son, and husband are distinguished according to their duties.

The Brahman in the Graveyard

The goblin told this story as he was being carried by King Vikram: "Along the river Kalindi there was a city named Brahmapura [Brahma's City]. In that city lived a brahman* named

---

* The classical caste system in India is comprised of the (a) brahman or priest; (b) kshatriya or ruler/warrior; (c) vaishya or farmer/merchant; and (d) shudra or servant birth groups.

16

Agnisvamin and his daughter, Mandaravati [Rich in Coral]. Seeing her beauty as equal to that of the heavens and the earth, three young priestly suitors asked her father for her hand in marriage. Her father responded, 'All three of you are handsome and wealthy as well as noted for your good families and masculine qualities. To which of you should I give my daughter?'

"One young brahman said, 'Give her to me.'

"Another young brahman responded, 'If this young woman is given to one of us worthy suitors, the other two will surely die. Then you would be guilty of murder.'

"Fearful of the terrible consequences of murdering a priest, Agnisvamin did not give his daughter to any of the three young brahmans.

"As fate would have it, Mandaravati died within a very short time. When she had been cremated, one of the young priests smeared his body with ashes from her funeral pyre and, wearing the matted hair and bark garments of an ascetic, went away into another country. The second young priest took her bones to various places of pilgrimage to receive blessings for her. The third young priest made himself a dwelling place upon the ashes of the cremation site and, abandoning wordly attachments, dwelt constantly on that spot.

"The first young brahman, wandering as an ascetic, came upon the house of a fellow brahman named Rudrasharman where he asked for food. Rudrasharman said to his wife, 'Give some food to this noble ascetic.' While the wife was cooking the meal, her son cried until, distraught, the wife threw her child into the fire. When the visiting brahman saw that the child had been killed and would be part of his meal he prepared to leave without taking any of the polluted food. Seeing his guest about to depart, Rudrasharman recited a magical incantation and brought his son back to life. The host ran after the ascetic to show him that the boy was alive and to prevent his going. After the young priest had returned and eaten the food, he took the book containing the charm and rushed back to Mandaravati's cremation site.

17

"In a short while, the second brahman suitor returned to the cremation ground with the bones of his beloved which he had washed at various places of pilgrimage. The third brahman still continued to guard the cremation site. Then the ascetic brahman took the bones and ashes from the other two suitors and formed a new body for Mandaravati which he brought to life by chanting the spell from the stolen book of charms. When they saw her restored to life, the three young brahmans all desired her more than ever and quarreled over whom she should marry."

The goblin asked King Vikram, "Who is her husband according to what is right?" Although desiring to remain quiet, the king gave this resolution: "Goblin, the one who possessed the charm is her *father* because he created her. The one who washed her bones at places of pilgrimage is her *son* because he cared for her when she was in the heavenly abode. The one who guarded the pyre and ashes is her true *husband* because he waited for her."

⁓

According to King Vikram, it is the father's duty (with his wife) to provide children to populate the family cluster. Therefore, the man who initiates life is the father. In agreement with religious tradition, King Vikram asserts that it is the son's duty to perform all the necessary rituals associated with death. Such activity is simply an extension of the filial task of honoring and caring for parents. The husband's role, however, is understood to encompass protection and care centered upon the wife during her lifetime. Consequently, the man who lived upon the funeral pyre represented the protection and honor accorded a wife with whom one lives daily.

The story of Nala which follows gives a contrasting glimpse of a man who fails in his husbandly duties.

18

Good King Nala's Downfall

The land of the Nishadhas was ruled by the handsome and strong King Nala. This young king possessed uncommon skills as a warrior, was a masterful horseman, and loved the game of dice. He stood above all kings in his generosity to holy men and in the protection of the citizens of his realm. He was learned in the religious traditions of his ancestors and endowed with all the good qualities of manhood. No man alive could match the wisdom, might, or goodness of King Nala.

In the nearby kingdom of Vidarbha there lived a young princess named Damayanti. Her beauty and virtue matched that of Nala, and when the time came for Damayanti to choose her husband even the gods of heaven came hoping to be chosen by this pretty maiden. In spite of the divine competition, Nala was chosen by Damayanti to be her husband.* It seemed the perfect marriage had been sealed.

As the gods returned home from the wedding of Nala and Damayanti they encountered on the road the evil god Kali† who was on the way to Damayanti's husband-choosing ceremony hoping to gain her hand in marriage. When he heard the ceremony had already taken place and that King Nala had been chosen, the evil Kali vowed to disrupt this perfect marriage. Though the other celestials told Kali that Nala would prevail in the end, the angry god vowed revenge.

For twelve years Nala and Damayanti lived in perfect harmony and love in accordance with their virtuous qualities. Then one morning Nala gave the evil Kali his chance to interfere. Forgetting to wash his feet before beginning his morning prayers [a breach in ritual preparation], Nala was immediately possessed by the spirit of Kali.

---

* See "An Act of Truth" in Chapter 3 for Damayanti's husband-choosing ceremony.
† In one ancient Indian dice game, Kali was the name of the losing die, which had one spot. Here Kali is personified.

19

In a weakened moral and intellectual state, Nala accepted the greedy king Pushkara's challenge to gamble. Aided by Kali, Pushkara sought to debase and dethrone Nala through a fateful game of dice.

The widely publicized game began even though Damayanti and the citizens of Nishadha tried to dissuade Nala from playing with the infamous Pushkara. Nala insisted that he could not refuse a public challenge, issued before his very wife as a witness. As the game of dice began behind the closed doors of Nala's palace, the influence of Kali was immediately apparent. Nala lost one fateful roll after another. First, his gold and silver were lost, then one by one all his material possessions. Nala's chariots and horses, his cows, his granaries, and finally, even his royal robes were lost to Pushkara. Though Damayanti, the court ministers, and the citizens of his kingdom all pleaded with him to stop the game, Nala persisted until he had bet his very kingdom, and lost. Then Pushkara insisted Nala offer Damayanti as a final prize, but Nala refused. Since Nala had nothing left to wager, Pushkara threw him out of the palace and banished him from his former realm.

Wandering in the forest with only one piece of cloth to wear and with his wife dutifully at his side, Nala sought roots and berries on which he and his wife could survive. Days passed, and the former king and queen both grew lean from hunger. One day Nala happened upon a small flock of birds that were unaware of his presence and he saw a chance for a meat dinner. He removed his single piece of cloth and cast it upon the birds as a makeshift fowler's net. The frightened birds flew up with Nala's only garment in tow. The debasement of the virtuous former king was complete as he stood nude in the forest.

Later Nala and Damayanti collapsed from fatigue and hunger in an abandoned hut in the forest. During the night, Nala awoke, cut off part of Damayanti's garment to cover himself, and, leaving his devoted wife asleep in the hut, set out alone through the forest. Twice he returned to the hut and twice departed, convincing himself that his beautiful wife would be better off without him. He reasoned that a maiden of her virtue would be protected from any danger the forest or its inhabitants could offer. He said to himself, "Should I desert my wife? Truly she is devoted to me and suffers distress on account of my actions. Freed of me, she may return to her relatives and enjoy once again the royal environment she deserves. If I do not leave her, Damayanti's devotion to me will only cause her further pain and suffering." So Nala abandoned Damayanti, who continued her exhausted sleep.

As morning approached, Damayanti awoke to find Nala gone. Crying out in anguish, Damayanti sobbed, "Oh my lord! Oh my dearest husband, why have you deserted me? Illustrious prince, if you are truthful and virtuous, how then can you desert me asleep in this fearful forest? I have been faithful to you and have done you no wrong, why then have you abandoned your husbandly duty of protection? I am so afraid! Please cease your terrible game and show yourself to me!" With these words Damayanti fell down sobbing at her predicament. After it was clear that Nala was not going to return, Damayanti set out in search of her husband.

While searching for Nala, Damayanti walked even deeper into the forest and encountered a huge serpent which encoiled her. Once again Damayanti called out to Nala for protection. A passing hunter heard her cries and came to her rescue. After killing the snake, the hunter learned of Damayanti's plight. Tempted by her beauty and her defenselessness, the hunter attempted to force himself on Damayanti. Calling upon her accumulated virtue, Damayanti cursed the hunter and he fell dead from the power of her words. As Damayanti wandered farther into the dark woods, she encountered one frightening situation after another until she finally came upon a caravan. Joining the caravan in hopes of getting out of the forest, Damayanti was welcomed by the merchants who pitied the near-starved woman.

The caravan leaders decided to stop for the night by a serene lake. As they set up camp along the shoreline, they were unaware that they were bedding down on the only route of access by which animals could approach the lake to drink and bathe. During the night, a large elephant herd charged the sleeping caravan, enraged at this obstacle in their path. Many deaths and injuries were the result of the elephants' charge through the sleeping camp. As the caravan leaders regrouped their remaining people and animals, they blamed their misfortune on their new traveling companion, Damayanti. Accused of being a witch or demoness in disguise, Damayanti was again set loose in the forest to find her own way.

After months of traveling alone, surviving only on the berries and roots she could find, Damayanti emerged from the forest a mere skeleton of flesh and bones. Coming upon a great city, Damayanti was taken in by the queen of that city and nursed back to health. Search parties of soldiers and priests were dispatched to seek Damayanti's possessed husband. It was through one of the priests who returned from a distant city that Damayanti learned that her husband also had encountered many hardships and had been deformed by a snake bite. Using the strategy of a second husband-choosing ceremony, Damayanti enticed Nala to come to the city in which she now lived. She asked Nala (now in the guise of Vahuka, a charioteer) what she had done to deserve being abandoned in the forest. Nala replied, "Oh frail one, neither the loss of my kingdom nor my abandonment of you were my acts. Both were due to Kali. I was possessed by that evil one and forced by him to do all those evil acts which led to your discomfort. That evil one has now left me, and I am here to reclaim your hand." Damayanti reaffirmed her original choice of Nala, and as Nala put on royal robes again, his disfiguration disappeared.

As is often the case in Indian tales, it is the husband, not the wife, who is pictured as a weak-willed person. Not only does Nala neglect his primary duty of protection when he abandons

Damayanti, but it is his wife's merit and persistence which in the end provides a happy reunion. Of course the storyteller provides the excuse that an angry god possessed Nala and made him show passion for dice and disregard for his wife's well-being. Still, that explanation does not excuse the misperformance of Nala's religious duty which gave the angry god his entrée. The householder's role, as that of men in general, is ideally superior to those of women and children. However, less than ideal performance of those masculine roles is evident throughout Indian literature.

Buddhist Stories

Indian stories unabashedly describe the husband as the head of the household. As such, he has to take responsibility for the moral behavior of all members of the household. In the following story we hear of a man who was only able to fulfill this role after getting some instruction from his precocious son. Note in the story how family members have the responsibility to carry out their roles properly even if the other members of the family are ungrateful, hostile, or negligent in their duties. The main thrust of the story is that a man must take care of his aged father, but the duties of the wife are also made clear.

The Wisdom of a Child

Once when Brahmadatta was king of Banaras there lived in a village of that region an old man and his only son, whose name was Vassitthako. Each day the son would get up very early and do the work normally delegated to women, such as preparing water and toothsticks with which the father could cleanse his mouth. Then the son would do manual labor all day, and finally he would bring home food and prepare it for his father. Finally his elderly father said, "Son, you have too much work to do. I

23

will get a wife for you who can do the housework and then you will only need to do your work outside the house."

"No, please don't do that," the son objected, "for if we bring a woman into the house we will have no peace of mind at all." But the father did not listen. He contracted for a bride, who soon came to live with them.

At first all was well, as the wife did her work and the son was relieved of his double responsibility. Then the new wife grew weary of waiting hand and foot upon the old man. She began deliberately to provoke the old man's wrath and then complain to her husband about it. After she had caused him to lose his temper several times, she confronted her husband with the problem, saying, "Look how your father makes a mess of this place, and he is always yelling at me. Husband, your father is a violent old man. I cannot live in the same house as he does. He is decrepit and is going to die soon anyway, so take him out to the burial ground, dig a grave, put him in it, hit him over the head with the spade, and bury the old man."

After repeated encounters such as that, the son finally agreed to get rid of his father, but said, "Wife, it is a serious crime to kill a man. How can I do it?"

"Here is a plan," she said. "First, go to him early one morning and speak to him in a voice loud enough for the neighbors to hear, saying that you want to take him to another village the next day to collect an old debt of his. Once you are away from town, dig the hole and bury him and then come back pretending that robbers attacked you on the road." The man agreed to this plan and all went well except that their young son overheard them plotting, and he devised his own plan for saving his beloved grandfather.

When the man put the grandfather in the cart, on the pretense of going to another village, the son got into the cart too. When they reached the burial ground and the man began to dig a hole, the boy asked, "Father, we have no bulbs or herbs for planting, no reason to dig a hole, so why are we out here digging?" The

24

father gave the gruesome explanation to the boy, but pretended it was a mercy killing, considering the grandfather's senility.

The grandson was not so easily fooled, however, and he condemned the act as cruel and sinful. He then took a spade and began to dig another hole near where his father was digging. "What are you doing?" the startled father asked. The boy replied, "I also will bury my father when he is old, since it is the family custom, so I might as well dig the hole now!"

"What a horrible thing to say to your own father," the man complained. "You are a foul-mouthed boy."

"I am not foul-mouthed or cruel, father, but I must speak my mind now for it will be soon too late. If a person kills his innocent father or mother, his next life will surely be in hell. But if a person feeds and cares for his elderly parents, just as surely he will be reborn in a heavenly world."

Upon hearing these wise words from his son, the man had a change of heart and apologized to his son. "It was your mother who put me up to this," he explained.

"That wife of yours, who gave me birth, is no good. You should send her out of the house before she causes another evil deed," the boy warned. His father took the advice. He returned home with the grandfather, and to his wife's horror, he beat her and expelled her from the house.

The wife lived at a neighbor's for several years until the son, now nearly grown, tricked her into thinking that her husband was going to remarry. Repentant and afraid for her livelihood, the woman begged to be taken back as a wife. She kept her promises and was a faithful housewife for the rest of her life. The family followed the advice of the wise young son, giving alms and doing good deeds, and eventually they all were rewarded in heaven.

These Hindu and Buddhist stories about men have emphasized the duty of protection—protection of one's wife, elderly parents, children, and all others living in the household. They also have revealed the image of male dominance that is common to the Indian household. We now turn to stories about women and their family roles.

WOMAN
Hindu Stories

The status and the image of women in India have always been fraught with ambivalence. On one hand, women are considered to be passionate creatures who know no bounds in their quest to satisfy their lust, and on the other hand, they are considered the bodily manifestations of the divine, creative feminine energy (*shakti*), which is often personified by the goddess who is "mother of all." In accord with the first perception of women, it is the men in a family (father, husband, and son) who are responsible for the helpless women of the house. A *Laws of Manu* text (9.2, 3) says bluntly, "Day and night women must be kept in dependence by the males of their families and must be kept under male control if they desire to express their passionate nature. A father protects a woman in her youth, her husband in her middle years, and her son in her old age; a woman is never fit for independence."

The common picture of a wife's role is that of a fully obedient servant to her husband. This subservient role is presented quite clearly in the statement, "If a wife is obedient to her husband, that alone will ensure her birth in heaven" (*Manu 5.155*). However, because a woman as mother and life-giver may be revered as the Mother Goddess herself, the same text (*Laws of Manu*) which derides women as morally deficient also says, "Where women are honored, the gods themselves rejoice, but where women are not honored, no religious act bears fruit" (3.56).

In the first tale which follows, the incorrigible passion of

26

women is displayed, but it is the second story, of the ideal wife Savatri, which is told and cherished in all parts of India by men and women alike.

The Carpenter's Wife

In a small town there was a carpenter whose lovely wife was as unfaithful as the carpenter's friends and family reported. In order to determine the truth of these rumors, the carpenter said to his wife one day, "My dear, there is a palace to be constructed in a distant city and I must go there to work. I will leave tomorrow and will spend a number of days there. Please make some food for my journey." The carpenter's wife joyfully prepared the provisions her husband requested. Early in the morning while it was still dark, the carpenter took his knapsack of provisions and said to his wife, "I am going, my dear, please lock the door." Instead of leaving, the carpenter circled his house, came in the back door and situated himself and his apprentice under his own bed.

The carpenter's wife was overjoyed at the thought that she could meet her paramour with no fear of being caught by her husband. She quickly summoned her lover through a close friend and the lovers ate and drank a meal together as though they were children freed from parental guidance. When they climbed into bed the wife's foot brushed against her husband's knee as he lay coiled up under the bed. Terrified, the wife thought, "Without a doubt, that must be my husband! What can I do?" Just then her lover asked, "Tell me dear, whom do you love more, me or your husband?"

The quick-witted wife responded, "What a silly question to ask. As you know, we women are accused of being immoral creatures who resort to all kinds of activities to satisfy our natural longings. In fact, some men would claim that we women would eat cow dung if we did not have noses to smell. But I would die on the spot if I should hear of any harm coming to my dear husband."

The carpenter was deceived by the lying words of his shameless wife, and he said to his apprentice, "Long live my beloved and fully devoted wife! I will praise her before all the people of the town." As he spoke, the carpenter rose up with the bed on his back, bearing his wife and her lover through the streets of the town proclaiming his wife to be devoted and honorable. And all of the people of the town laughed at the foolish carpenter.

The above well-known tale from the *Panchatantra* expresses only the negative view of women, as passion-filled, deceitful creatures. At the other extreme, the story of Savatri not only pictures a devoted wife and daughter-in-law but a bold and courageous person as well.

Savatri and the God of Death

Ashvapati, the virtuous king of Madras, grew old without offspring to continue his royal family. Desiring a son, Ashvapati took rigid vows and observed long fasts to accumulate merit. It is said that he offered 10,000 oblations to the goddess Savatri in hopes of having a son. After eighteen years of constant devotion, Ashvapati was granted his wish for an offspring even though the baby born was a girl.

The king rejoiced at his good fortune and named the child Savatri in honor of the goddess who gave him this joy to brighten his elder years.

Savatri was both a beautiful and an intelligent child. She was her father's delight and grew in wisdom and beauty as the years passed. As the age approached for Savatri to be given in marriage as custom demanded, no suitor came forward to ask her father for her hand—so awed were all the princes by the beauty and intellect of this unusual maiden. Her father became concerned lest he not fulfill his duty as a father and incur disgrace for his failure to provide a suitable husband for his daughter. At last, he instructed Savatri herself to lead a procession throughout the surrounding kingdoms and handpick a man suitable for her.

Savatri returned from her search and told her father that she had found the perfect man. Though he was poor and an ascetic of the woods, he was handsome, well educated, and of kind temperament. His name was Satyavan and he was actually a prince whose blind father had been displaced by an evil king. Ashvapati asked the venerable sage Narada whether Satyavan would be a suitable spouse for Savatri. Narada responded that there was no one in the world more worthy than Satyavan. However, Narada continued, Satyavan had one unavoidable flaw. He was fated to live a short life and would die exactly one year from that very day. Ashvapati then tried to dissuade Savatri from marrying Satyavan by telling her of the impending death of her loved one. Savatri held firm to her choice, and the king and Narada both gave their blessings to this seemingly ill-fated bond.

After the marriage procession had retreated from the forest hermitage of Savatri's new father-in-law, Dyumatsena, the bride removed her wedding sari and donned the ocher robe and bark garments of her ascetic family. As the days and weeks passed, Savatri busied herself by waiting upon the every need of her new family. She served her husband, Satyavan, cheerfully and skillfully. Satyavan responded with an even-tempered love which enhanced the bond of devotion between Savatri and himself. Yet the dark cloud of Narada's prophecy cast a shadow over this otherwise blissful life.

When the fateful time approached, Savatri began a fast to strengthen her wifely resolve as she kept nightly vigils while her husband slept. The day marked for the death of Satyavan began as any other day at the hermitage. Satyavan shouldered his axe and was about to set off to cut wood for the day's fires when Savatri stopped him to ask if she could go along saying, "I can-

29

not bear to be separated from you today." Satyavan responded, "You've never come into the forest before and the paths are rough and the way very difficult. Besides, you've been fasting and are surely weak." Savatri persisted, and Satyavan finally agreed to take her along. Savatri went to her parents-in-law to get their permission saying she wanted to see the spring blossoms which now covered the forest. They too expressed concern over her health but finally relented out of consideration for her long period of gracious service to them.

Together Satyavan and Savatri entered the tangled woods enjoying the beauty of the flowers and animals which betoken spring in the forest. Coming to a fallen tree, Satyavan began chopping firewood. As he worked, he began to perspire heavily and to grow weak. Finally, he had to stop and lie down telling Savatri to wake him after a short nap. With dread in her heart, Savatri took Satyavan's head in her lap and kept a vigil knowing Satyavan's condition to be more serious than rest could assuage. In a short time, Savatri saw approaching a huge figure clad in red and carrying a small noose. Placing Satyavan's head upon the ground, Savatri arose and asked the stranger of his mission. The lord of death replied, "I am Yama and your husband's days are finished. I speak to you, a mortal, only because of your extreme merit. I have come personally instead of sending my emissaries because of your husband's righteous life."

Without a further word, Yama then pulled Satyavan's soul out of his body with the small noose he was carrying. The lord of death then set off immediately for the realm of the dead in the south. Grief stricken and yet filled with wifely devotion, Savatri followed Yama at a distance. Hours passed yet hunger and weariness could not slow Savatri's footsteps. She persisted through thorny paths and rocky slopes to follow Yama and his precious burden. As Yama walked south he thought he heard a woman's anklets tingling on the path behind him. He turned around to see Savatri in the distance following without pause. He called out to her to return to Satyavan's body and to perform her wifely du-

ties of cremating the dead. Savatri approached Yama and responded, "It is said that those who walk seven steps together are friends. Certainly we have traveled farther than that together. Why should I return to a dead body when you possess the soul of my husband?"

Yama was impressed by the courage and wisdom of this beautiful young woman. He replied, "Please stop following me. Your wise words and persistent devotion for your husband deserve a boon. Ask of me anything except that your husband's life be restored, and I will grant it." Savatri asked that her blind father-in-law be granted new sight. Yama said that her wish would be granted, and then he turned to leave only to find that Savatri was about to continue following. Yama again praised her devotion and offered a second, and then a third boon. Savatri told Yama of the misfortune of her father-in-law's lost kingdom and asked that Yama assist in ousting the evil king from Dyumatsena's throne. Yama agreed. Then Savatri utilized her third boon to ask that her own father be given one hundred sons to protect his royal line, and that too was granted by Yama.

Yama then set off in a southerly direction only to discover after a short while that Savatri still relentlessly followed him. Yama was amazed at the thoroughly self-giving attitude displayed by Savatri and agreed to grant one last boon if Savatri would promise to return home. Yama again stipulated that the bereaved wife could not ask for her husband's soul. Savatri agreed to the two conditions and said, "I only ask for myself one thing, and that is that I may be granted one hundred sons to continue Satyavan's royal family." Yama agreed only to realize, upon prompting from Savatri, that the only way Satyavan's line could be continued would be for him to be restored to life. Although he had been tricked by the wise and thoughtful Savatri, Yama laughed heartily and said, "So be it! Auspicious and chaste lady, your husband's soul is freed by me." Loosening his noose Yama permitted the soul of Satyavan to return to its earthly abode and Savatri ran without stopping back to the place where Satyavan had fallen asleep. Just as Savatri arrived at the place where her husband lay, he awoke saying, "Oh, I have slept into the night, why did you not waken me?"

Many other famous legendary wives (such as Damayanti and Sita, whose faithfulness will be recounted in the story "A Test of Fire") are more like Savatri than the carpenter's wife, leaving a vivid impression that Indian women are more often honored for their loyalty and courage than scorned for their lustful natures. Certainly the ritual practice, now forbidden, in which a widow ascended her husband's funeral pyre to share his fate indicated the extent to which some women took their wifely duties of dependence and devotion. Still, ascetics and other religious figures feared the passion they saw in—or projected upon—women, leaving the Hindu image of women ambiguous at best.

Buddhist Stories

The same ambiguous image of women runs through the Buddhist stories. The Buddhists idealized the ascetic life, which required leaving the comforts of home and the pleasures of women's company, so it is not surprising that wives and women get a negative review in most of the Buddhist stories. Where they are presented favorably, we find them also departing the world and living as ascetics or members of Buddha's Order (*Sangha*).

We will begin with a Buddhist story of a model wife, along the lines of the Hindu story of Savatri. Then we will present a story with an extremely negative image of women. The third story is about the disturbances in men which beautiful women can cause, whether or not they intend to.

The Radiant Sambula

Once King Brahmadatta had a son named Sotthisena, who was appointed viceroy when he matured. Sotthisena's chief wife was an extraordinarily beautiful and virtuous woman named Sambula. Her beauty was as radiant as the flame of a lamp.

All was well for a while, but then Sotthisena contracted incurable leprosy. It became so bad that he decided to renounce the throne, depart from the world, and live out his remaining days as a hermit ascetic. The king and the other wives let him depart alone, for his open sores were becoming foul and rotten. However, Sambula insisted that she accompany him wherever he might go, saying, "I will take care of you in the forest, husband." So they went together into the forest where the man built a leaf hut in a pleasant spot.

Sambula dedicated herself totally to caring for her ever worsening husband. She rose before him in the morning and prepared water and a toothstick for him. She gathered fruit and vegetables for his food and bathed his wretched skin with cooling water. One day as she gathered food deep in the forest, she noticed a pleasant pool in a cave and bathed herself there. As she put on her bark clothing again and stepped from the cave, her radiance lit up the dark forest. This attracted the attention of an ogre who happened to reside in the area, and he immediately wanted her as his chief consort. She refused the seven-fanged monster of course, explaining that she was devoted to Prince Sotthisena who depended upon her for his food and water. The ogre gave her one more chance to marry him and then seized her and prepared to make a meal of her. She struggled but was helpless against the ogre's strength. Her spiritual power was so great, however, from many years of virtuous actions that the yellow throne of the god Sakka began to heat up. Then, as usual when his throne heats up, Sakka immediately came to earth to see what person of great merit was causing this threat to his rule as king of the gods.

Thunderbolt in hand, Sakka approached the ogre and spoke to him of Sambula's great virtue. He warned the ogre that if he did eat the radiant Sambula, his head would split into seven pieces, and advised him to let her return to her husband, which the ogre did. Sakka took the ogre to a place far away and then returned to his heavenly throne.

Meanwhile Sambula returned very late to her leprous husband in the forest hut. Her husband heard her singing a lament as she approached, and he became suspicious, asking pointedly, "Why are you so late, famous princess? Who did you pass the time with, my precious?"

Sambula told of how she had become the object of an ogre's affection and how she had escaped only with the help of Sakka himself. But the suspicious Sotthisena continued to mistrust her and reminded her of the wiles of women. "Oh my husband," she sighed in desperation, "what can I do to convince you of my devotion to you alone?" Then the solution occurred to her. She would perform the ancient ritual called an "Act of Truth" [in which a person of great virtue proclaims the basis of the virtue and, if the claim be true, the power of the virtue will prove sufficient to work any miracle requested]. So she proclaimed aloud, "May I be protected by this truth; that I have never held anyone dearer than you. By this spoken truth, may your disease be cured." To complete the ritual she poured water over the diseased skin of her husband and immediately his sores were washed away.

They remained a few days longer as ascetics and then the prince decided to return to the worldly life. Having heard the news that his son was returning in good health, the old king met the prince at the entrance to the city and ordered two rituals to be performed. First he had the royal parasol raised over Sotthisena's head, which is the traditional Indian way of enthroning a king. Then he had the priests perform a ritual in which they sprinkled Sambula with holy water and elevated her to the office of "Chief Wife of the King." Then the old king retired to the forest to live an ascetic's life in preparation for death, according to Indian tradition.

As the years passed the new king merely acknowledged Sambula's official position as chief wife, while in fact he ignored her and preferred to spend his time with the younger girls in his harem. Sambula bore the insult in silence; but the hurt and jealousy caused her to lose her appetite, and she grew thin and frail.

One day when the retired king came to the palace for food he noticed Sambula's sad state and asked what could be worrying her, for she lived in total security within the palace walls. She explained her plight to the old king, who had a serious talk with her husband, saying, "A good husband or wife is very hard to find. But you have a wife who is very virtuous, so treat Sambula according to righteousness (*dharma*)." The husband apologized to Sambula and promised that he and the other wives would pay her the honor she deserved. Sambula and the king lived happily and virtuously together at court for many years. Eventually they died and were rewarded because of their merit, and the old king, having found peace through meditation, went to the realm of the god Brahma after he died.

⁓

Now we turn to a story which presents the negative view of women as slaves to passion, especially sexual lust. (Also note the role of the king as commander in chief, administrator of justice, and head of the court, which will be the subject of several stories in the next chapter.)

The Queen Who Cried Rape

Once when Brahmadatta was king of Banaras the Future Buddha (Bodhisattva) was born into the family of the brahman who held the post of king's chaplain. Eventually the Future Buddha succeeded his father as king's chaplain. The king was very pleased with his chief wife and granted her one boon. She said, "What I wish is not difficult to fulfill: I wish that you would never again look upon another woman with love." The king refused the re-

36

quest at first, for he had many women in his harem, but the queen persisted until he granted her request.

Some time later a robber band was causing trouble in a rural part of the kingdom and the king's frontier police could not stop them, so the king himself led an army against the robbers. Before he left, the queen made him promise to send back a messenger to report to her every day the king marched. On the way out to the field of battle thirty-two messengers were sent back to the queen, and the same number on the return. By her beauty and her position of authority she seduced each messenger—sixty-four in all!

When the king and the army were nearly back to the city a message came to the chaplain to alert the city and prepare for a triumphal entry. The handsome chaplain went to the queen with the news. She saw this as an opportunity for yet another seduction. But the chaplain was a man of impeccable virtue, and he refused. "You must be afraid of the king," she chided, and added, "The sixty-four other messengers were not."

"The other messengers do not think as I do," he responded. "I have never stolen anything, drunk strong liquor, nor made love to another man's wife, and I never will."

"Do you forget that I am the queen," she said menacingly, "and I can have you beheaded if you do not do what I want?" "If you must," he responded as he left her and continued his work. The angry queen decided to take revenge. She scratched herself and pretended to be ill. When the king came to inquire about her illness, she coyly waited until he asked three times and then sobbed that the chaplain had tried to rape her in the king's absence.

The angered king ordered the immediate beheading of the chaplain, but the chaplain managed to get a word with the king by pretending to know the location of some buried treasure. Once he had the ear of the king he told his side of the story and suggested that the king get the testimony of the sixty-four messengers.

Upon learning the truth the king ordered all the messengers and the queen beheaded. But the chaplain intervened. He said that the messengers were not to blame, for they were only obeying their queen, and asked for their pardon. As for the queen, he said, "No blame should be accounted to her, for women indeed are insatiable in sexual matters. She was only acting according to the nature of those born as women. Therefore, pardon her too."

Having avoided the loss of any life, the chaplain, with the wisdom of a Future Buddha, went on to instruct the king in the wisdom of following the counsel of the wise and not the foolish. Realizing that he would not have become an object of the queen's affection if he had not been living the worldly life, the chaplain withdrew from his family and possessions, and went to live the life of a forest ascetic. There he attained great spiritual wisdom and became destined for rebirth in the realm of the god Brahma.

From the ascetic point of view which underlies the previous story women are passionate creatures whose seductive powers are matched with promiscuity, making a deadly combination for any man who wishes to lead a virtuous life. Yet the prohibition referred specifically to the immorality of having sexual intercourse with another man's wife. Paying for the services of a professional prostitute was not considered evil by most persons in ancient India. We find in such stories as the following one that the profession of prostitution was quite accepted and that the prostitute in this story was rich, famous, and respected—more comparable to a movie star than the prostitute of contemporary Western society. What is condemned in the story is not prostitution but that some men, such as one young Buddhist monk, lose control at the sight of such great beauty. Buddha's solution to the problem is as imaginative as it is drastic.

The Prostitute Who Lost Her Charm

Once when the Buddha was teaching in the area of Rajagaha the famous prostitute of the area, Sirima, happened to visit a lay woman's house at the very time that the Buddha was giving instruction to lay people. Hearing some of the instruction from the Master, Sirima converted and became a devoted and generous supporter of the Buddhist Order of monks. With the wealth she had accumulated from her high-priced services Sirima was mistress of a mansion and many servants. Whenever Buddhist monks came by for alms she would personally serve them food fit for a king. Soon she became as famous for her food gifts to the monks as she had been for her sexual prowess among the laymen.

One young monk overheard another monk praise Sirima's food *and* physical appearance in great detail one night and determined to see her for himself. He arranged this on a day when she happened to be so seriously ill that her servants had to carry her on a cot to a point where she could salute the monks. The young monk fell hopelessly in love with her—even though she had been too weak to dress up properly in jewels and fine clothing. He was so lovesick that he did not eat for several days. During this time Sirima died and the king, at Buddha's request, had her nude body put on display at the burning grounds, rather than being cremated. Again acting upon Buddha's request, the king ordered all his subjects to view Sirima's decomposing, maggot-infested body. "Who will pay one thousand pieces of money for Sirima's body," the town criers called out. When there were no takers, the price was lowered and lowered and lowered until at last no one would have Sirima for free, though men had formerly paid one thousand a night! The lovesick monk was cured and the teaching of the Buddha about the transitoriness of all things, including a woman's beauty, was impressed upon the minds of the people of Rajagaha.

Buddhist stories have pictured a whole spectrum of women from the devoted ones who uphold their husbands and children through difficult times to the seductive, conniving women who cause trouble for men. There are also stories about women who are stingy or who are dissatisfied with the income provided by their husbands, stories about women who get drunk, and stories about women who run to their fathers or brothers too much to complain about their husbands. Yet there are stories about women whose generosity or wisdom far exceeds their husbands', while other women put up with the most despicable behavior on the part of the men in their lives. Typically Buddhist also are the stories about model women who depart from the secular life and enter into a religious life.

CHILDREN
Hindu Stories

In keeping with the high value of male roles in Indian society, a householder is obliged to produce not merely a child but a son. Consequently, in the early months of pregnancy it is customary for high-status Hindus to perform the ceremony of "acquiring a son." Nonetheless, daughters too may be thought to have exceptional value, as the following story indicates.

A Goddess Is Born

The powerful, world-ruling King Daksha was responsible for peopling the earth and, to that end, married a beautiful young woman named Virini. Together they bore 5000 sons whose job it was to sire all the people of the world. The 5000 sons set off on a journey to the west and engaged in severe penances to acquire the virility needed for their important task. While the sons of

41

Daksha were living by a lake and doing merit-making austerities, they were persuaded by the celestial sage Narada to renounce the world of birth and death and become permanent wandering ascetics.

When his sons did not return from their preparatory journey, Daksha and his wife produced yet another 1000 sons. When these 1000 sons had matured, Daksha sent them off with a warning about the fate of the earlier 5000, but the same end resulted. Grief stricken, Daksha cursed the sage Narada for depriving the world of its progenitors. Daksha's own father, Brahma, consoled him and encouraged him to try yet again to populate the earth through his progeny. Again Daksha and Virini copulated, only this time 60 daughters were born. As Daksha and Virini gazed upon their daughters, they meditated upon the mother of all creation, Durga-shakti, and with awe-filled words extolled the divine feminine creative force.

The goddess Durga was flattered and agreed to enter the world in the form of one of Daksha's daughters as a fulfillment of Daksha's desire to populate the earth. The usual signs of pregnancy alerted Virini that she would bear yet another child. When it came time for Daksha to perform [as his fatherly duty] the rite of "acquiring a son" unknown to the mother and father all the gods of heaven came to visit the Mother Goddess who was lodged firmly in the womb of Virini. To perceptive eyes, Virini's complexion radiated the presence of the in-dwelling goddess.

When nine months had passed and the moon, the stars, and the planets were in their most favorable alignment, the goddess who mothers all things was born in the form of the beautiful baby Sati. As the new daughter of Daksha and Virini entered the world, the heavens showered gentle rain and flowers. The gods in heaven rejoiced in music and song at the gift of life represented in the baby Sati. Recognizing his daughter's true nature, Daksha said to his newborn child, "Oh Goddess, the eternal mother of the universe, we bow down to you. Please accept our honoring you who are most true and truth-giving. I bow to you, the great goddess who creates all things living."

42

At that moment, the baby Sati stirred at the side of her mother Virini and began to cry. All the servants of the house gathered around the newborn baby and danced and sang with delight at the sight of the newborn daughter of Daksha and Virini.

As we saw in the stories in which a positive role is attributed to a wife and mother, the story of the birth of Sati demonstrates one positive way in which a family may view the birth of a daughter. While a son may be said to be preferred, many a happy Indian father has held his daughter to his chest thanking the goddess who gives all life for such a blessing.

The interdependent set of family responsibilities extends to brothers and sisters too. Since the joint family often includes several brothers and their families (sisters are usually spread out among their various husbands' homes), affection and consideration between brothers is very important, as is revealed in many Hindu tales. One such tale is that of the noble King Yudhishthira whose devotion to his brothers extended even into hell.

A Journey into Hell

As King Yudhishthira entered heaven he saw his cousin Duryodhana seated in regal splendor. Angry that his earthly enemy was the first person he saw in heaven, Yudhishthira said, "Oh gods of heaven, I have no wish to see Duryodhana! It was because of him that my friends and relatives by the hundreds were slaughtered in battle. I wish to go where my brothers are." The sage Narada responded, "You should not speak that way. Such bitterness has no place in heaven." Yudhishthira retorted to Narada and the celestials who had gathered around, "Oh gods of heaven, what is heaven to me if I am separated from my brothers? To me, heaven is where my brothers are. That is where I want to go."

Obligingly the gods ordered one of their messengers to take Yudhishthira to his friends and relatives, and the messenger set off with Yudhishthira following on a path which became darker and more foreboding as they went. The path was enveloped with slimy moss and the stench of rotting flesh and blood. The air surrounding the path was filled with stinging flies, gnats, and bees. Vultures and other large birds with beaks of iron hovered ominously above the path. Human corpses were scattered about the path, and many of them were missing arms or legs while others had spewed out their entrails upon the rocky trail.

At last the two travelers from heaven came upon a river running with boiling water. Beyond the river were forests of trees which had leaves sharp as razors and beyond which deserts of molton rocks stretched as far as the eye could see. Yudhishthira said to his guide, "Where are my brothers? How long must we travel this ill-bred path?" The messenger replied, "This is as far as I may go. I must now return to heaven. If you have tired of your quest, you may return with me." Tired of limb and soul, Yudhishthira decided that it was useless to go farther down the ill-omened trail. Just as he turned to retrace his steps, Yudhishthira heard wailing voices, "Oh royal sage, Oh you of sacred origin, O son of Pandu, please remain with us just a little while. At your approach a refreshing breeze had begun to blow. Your presence has brought us great relief, so please remain just a moment to give us some peace."

Hearing these words of anguish, Yudhishthira paused on the path. The voices which cried out pitifully seemed vaguely familiar though Yudhishthira could not quite recognize them. "Who are you? Why are you here?" he asked, and voices responded from all sides calling out the names of his family. Hearing his own brothers, wife, and friends call out to him, Yudhishthira lamented, "What perverse destiny is this? What sin of theirs was so great that they have been relegated to this place of stench and woe? And by what great merit do King Duryodhana and his followers enjoy the bliss of heaven?"

Yudhishthria cursed the gods of heaven for this display of injustice. Though nearly overcome by the stench of the hellish region, Yudhishthira said to the messenger, "Go back to heaven and tell your heavenly lords that I shall not return to them but shall instead remain here with my kinsmen and friends. My presence here seems to bring them relief."

In the wink of an eye, all the celestials, headed by Indra, appeared before Yudhishthira. Upon their arrival, the darkness and stench disappeared from the place where the rebellious king stood. Indra, the lord of the gods, spoke, "Oh mighty Yudhishthira, the illusion has ended. You may now join your brothers and friends in heaven. Hell should be seen by all kings since there is good and bad in all things. Like yourself, your brothers and friends reached hell by an illusion such as you experienced. They all have now attained their rightful places in heaven." The lord of virtue, Dharma, continued, "Your brothers did not deserve hell. All of this has been an illusion created by the god of illusion. Come now, righteous king, and follow me to the Ganges River which flows through all three worlds."

Yudhishthira then followed Dharma and the other gods to the banks of the heavenly Ganges River. Having bathed in the celestial portion of that sacred river, Yudhishthira left behind his material body. Assuming his celestial form, Yudhishthira forgot his anger, spite, and anguish and joined his brothers and previous enemies in heaven.

━━━

For Yudhishthira, his relationship with his brothers was more important than heaven itself. Such devotion to siblings and family is reported again and again in the tales of India. Another good example is that found in the epic tale of the *Ramayana* in which Lakshman is pictured as the fully devoted brother who follows King Rama into exile. The bond of family again serves as the primary relationship against which all other relationships and events are to be judged.

Buddhist Stories

The Buddhist stories also reflect the Indian preference for male children, without disparaging females. However, there are very few stories dealing with the theme of sibling solidarity, as found in the story of Yudhishthira. Instead, typical Buddhist stories illustrate these themes: children and spouses should not lament too much for deceased loved ones, a son or daughter has an absolute obligation to care for aged parents or grandparents, and departing the world is even more noble than being a faithful member of a family.

How a King Learned To Care for Parents

Once there were two hunters who lived in villages on opposite sides of the Ganges River. The son of one hunter had long been contracted in marriage to the daughter of the other. But when the son became old enough to marry, he refused to do so, saying that he preferred to depart from the householder life and become an ascetic. When the girl heard about her fiancé's decision, she announced her similar decision, so the young couple withdrew to the forest to live as celibate ascetics.

At their decision the god Sakka's throne grew hot, as it does when especially virtuous persons practice asceticism, and he descended to earth and built them a forest hermitage. All went well for many years, as Sakka watched over them; but Sakka foresaw their eventual blindness and recommended to them that they copulate to produce a son who could look after them when they became blind. They were aghast at the suggestion of practicing sexual intercourse, but Sakka worked a miraculous conception and they were relieved of having to lapse from their vows of celibacy.

A boy was born, and he was as virtuous as they. After the boy had matured the parents were indeed blinded by the venom of a snake, and when the boy found them floundering in the forest he both laughed and cried. When his parents asked about his curious response, he said that he wept because of their misfortune but he was happy for himself, for now he would have the opportunity to be of great service to his parents. From that day on he devoted himself entirely to their care. He brought them water and toothsticks in the morning, well-chosen fruits and vegetables during the day, and heated water for their bath in the evening.

One day as the boy was getting water, the king, who was on a hunt, saw the forest youth and shot him with a poison arrow, assuming that the boy was some supernatural creature. The boy bled and became stiff, but before losing consciousness he conversed with the king and lamented the fact that his parents would now have no caretaker. The king was so ashamed of himself and so impressed with the boy's filial devotion that he determined to renounce his throne and stay in the forest to care for the blind parents himself.

The blind parents received the king and were not angry at him for shooting their son. While grieving over the boy's body, however, the woman performed an Act of Truth and the power of her stated truth, plus that of her husband and a nearby goddess, miraculously restored the boy's life. The youth, who was in fact the Future Buddha in one of his previous lives, then instructed the king in the great value in taking care of one's parents, saying, "Those children who treat their mothers and fathers according to righteousness [dharma] please the gods and go to heaven when they die." The king accepted the duty of caring for one's parents and several other duties as well, and as a result of his meritorious living from that day forward, he was eventually rewarded in the heavenly world of Brahma.

Although the early Indian Buddhists valued family life and emphasized the responsibilities of children toward their aging parents, a great deal of tension existed between the family order and the Order of Buddhist monks. The reason for this was that the Buddhist teaching encouraged young men to leave home—parents, wife, even children at times—in order to pursue the spiritual path. This was at cross-purposes with traditional family values, which encouraged the young man to marry and raise children (especially sons) for the preservation of the family line.

The tension between Buddhist monastic ideals and family ideals was especially great when the family was a proud upper-class one or when an only son wished to become celibate before fathering any heirs. The son in the following story has to face both of these complications.

The Only-Child Who Left Home

During the many years in which Buddha traveled through northern India teaching in various cities and villages, he once came into a prosperous market town in the area where the Kuru people live. Nearly everyone from the village came to hear Buddha teach, and afterward a young man named Ratthapala saluted the Buddha and said, "As I understand your teaching, Lord, it is not easy for one who lives the householder life to make great progress on the godly path, the path to being as pure and polished as a well-rubbed conch shell. Lord, I wish to shave off my hair and beard, put on a saffron robe, and be admitted to your order of those who have gone forth from the householder life."

The Buddha asked, "Do you have the permission of your parents to go forth into the homeless life?" Ratthapala answered that he did not, and the Buddha explained that a Tathagata (another name for a Buddha) does not allow a youth to go forth without his parents' permission. The youth hastened to his parents and asked for such permission, and was told, "Dear Ratthapala, you are our beloved only son. You live very comfortably here and do not know suffering. Eat, drink, and be merry; and besides eating, drinking, and amusing yourself you can also perform meritorious acts while living as a householder. We cannot grant you permission to go forth as long as we are alive. If you were to die before we do, we would become joyless without you, so how can we give you permission to leave us?"

Ratthapala asked a second and a third time, but the parents insisted that his responsibility was to his family. Ratthapala then sat down on the ground and proclaimed, "I will either die here or go forth from here." From that moment on he refused to move, to eat, or to drink. His distraught parents made their speech to him again and again, but Ratthapala remained silent. The parents anxiously turned to his friends and asked them to come and speak on their behalf, but Ratthapala remained silent, all the while refusing to eat or drink.

The friends reported their lack of success to the parents and asked them to reconsider, suggesting that if they didn't he would die, but if allowed to go he might become discontent with the homeless life and return. The parents reluctantly conceded and the friends conveyed the good news to Ratthapala, adding, "But after you go forth, you must come back to see your parents."

With joyful expectation Ratthapala left behind his inheritance, friends, parents, and responsibilities as son, going forth to become a homeless Buddhist monk.

~~~~~

These Indian stories are told from a man's point of view. Men are seen as the proper head of the family, as the ones responsible for the welfare, protection, and morality of the family. However, men are capable of lapses of duty, as was the case with Nala and Vassitthako. According to these stories, when men fail in their family duties, it is often through some outside influence. For example, Nala was bewitched into gambling by an angry god and Vassitthako was led astray by his nagging wife.

Women in the stories are often pictured in extremes. Some women are like goddesses in beauty and devotion to their duty

49

(*dharma*). Conversely, in the stories originally told for the benefit of celibate ascetics (Buddhist or Hindu), the image of women is quite negative. Women are conniving, seductive, and lustful, these stories maintain. This ambiguity in the female image leaves the impression that, from the point of view of the classical Indian storyteller, women have an important role to play in the family, but their inherent weaknesses necessitate their being subordinate to men.

The stories are also told from an adult's point of view, and the dominant theme concerning children is that they should be obedient toward their parents and should take especially good care of aging parents. Appropriate rewards in heaven are promised for those who care for aging parents, with parallel punishments in hell for those who kill or abuse their parents.

We can conclude from these stories that for the Hindus and to a lesser extent the Buddhists the proper fulfillment of family roles was a *religious* duty. The gods are pleased with someone who follows his or her family dharma, and society as a whole benefits when the members of extended families live together in peaceful cooperation. This cooperation, as the stories reveal, is not based upon equality but upon a system of well-defined, interdependent roles for each family member. Other stories make clear the roles of all the members of the extended household, such as widows, second wives, unmarried younger brothers, and others. Having the duty (*dharma*) of each member of the family spelled out so carefully might seem to be a severe restriction upon individual freedom, but some Hindus and Buddhists would argue that structured social roles facilitate spiritual growth.

2
Social Roles

In one hymn from Vedic India (*c.* 800 B.C.), a divine man is used as a mythic model for the creation of the world and of humans in four classes. In that creation story (*Rig Veda*, X. 90) the priest (*brahmana*) is said to have come from the *mouth* of the divine man, the warrior/king from his two mighty *arms*, the producer (merchants and traders) from his *thighs*, and the servant from his *feet*. This priestly story suggests a social pecking order, and it in fact broadly outlines the so-called caste system of classical and contemporary India. While there have been squabbles among the priest and warrior/king groups as to which of the two really resides at the top of the social ladder, tradition and practice clearly place the producers third and servants fourth, as in the ancient myth.

While the social system that has dominated Indian history has been hierarchical, the various social groups have had reciprocal responsibilities. For example, the priests should serve as the spiritual and vocational instructors of all other castes (giving special attention to the instruction and support of the kings), while the rulers must protect all the people of their realm (especially the priests and their rituals). In addition to these official responsibilities, certain stereotypes became attached to the public roles of king and priest, providing images of the way people *do* live and models for the way they *ought* to live.

The Buddhist tradition deemphasizes the caste system, yet it abounds in stories about the special roles of social leaders such as kings, teachers, and ascetics. The practice of correct behavior by and toward such persons is a very important part of Buddhist morality, which in turn is considered a necessary first step before great progress in meditation and wisdom are possible.

Here then are some Buddhist and Hindu stories which present images of and models for the social roles of king, teacher/priest, and ascetic.

KING
Hindu Stories

According to the traditional role of the king, it is the warrior/king's responsibility "to protect the whole world." The king carries the staff of power in order to punish those who disobey his law and to war against those who would threaten his people and rule from without. In the story that follows we observe this protective function in the divine-king Krishna, an emanation of the god Vishnu.

The Serpent with One Hundred Heads

The serpent Kaliya lived in the river Kalindi, nearby Krishna's cowherd home. No ordinary serpent, Kaliya had one hundred heads and the poison of as many snakes. Kaliya's venom had affected all the territory surrounding his watery home. Birds would drop from the sky killed by the poisonous air which hung thick

తాండవకృష్ణా
కృష్ణుడు
కాళింగుణ్ణి
సంహారించాడు

above the river. The grass and trees along the river had long since withered and died, and the water of the river could kill the heartiest man or beast.

Once Krishna and his friends were tending their cows not far from the river Kalindi and, having become thirsty in the noonday sun, drank some of the poisoned water. Seeing his friends fall dead, Krishna exerted his divine powers and gave back life to his cowherd companions. Recognizing that the serpent Kaliya was the source of the poison, Krishna climbed the only surviving tree on the riverbank and dived into the water. Krishna thrashed about in the water and made such a disturbance that Kaliya surfaced and encircled the young cowherder in his strong coils, seeking to squeeze the life from his tormentor. In the tussle which ensued, it appeared that Krishna was losing the battle. The earth erupted with violent quakes. Meteors shot across the sky, and peoples' limbs shook from no apparent cause. Friends and relatives from Krishna's village of Vraja came running to see what could be causing these dramatic signs.

Seeing the plight of Krishna, all those on the riverbank sought to drown themselves . . . not wanting to live without their most beloved friend. Only the strong arm of Balarama, Krishna's older brother, prevented the drownings. Seeing his friends in such dismay, Krishna ceased his pretending and expanded his chest, breaking the grip of Kaliya's coils. Enraged, Kaliya rose out of the water and breathed fire in an attempt to destroy Krishna. Krishna responded by leaping from the water onto one of the hundred hoods of Kaliya and dancing upon it until blood replaced venom as the product of its hollow tongue. One by one, the one hundred heads of Kaliya were danced into submission until the huge serpent lay unconscious in the water.

Everyone cheered, except the wives of Kaliya who pleaded for their husband's life. Out of compassion, Krishna banished Kaliya and his wives to an ocean far from the villages of his friends. Kaliya and his wives departed, praising the compassionate Lord Krishna.

The story of Kaliya and Krishna is depicted in Indian sculpture, painting, and poetry as an example of the divine protection of the loving and merciful god Vishnu from whom Krishna descended as a human manifestation. The duty of protection for the warrior/king is clear in this story, as is the warrior's use of power in the defeat of his foes. The next story, however, is an animal fable which counsels a different kingly virtue for the ruler who is weaker than his foes.

The Wise Old Crow

Once upon a time in a certain forest there was a large banyan tree. In that tree lived a crow king named Cloudcolor with his following of one thousand crows. In that same forest an owl king named Foe-crusher lived with one thousand owls who served him. One night, given the natural enmity between owls and crows, Foe-crusher led his forces in a devastating attack upon the sleeping crows. Early the next morning, Cloudcolor gathered together those crows who had escaped the owl attack and sought advice from his counselors as to the crows' proper response.

One advisor suggested retreating to a new forest. Another preferred remaining and making peace with the owls. Still another recommended a pendulum-like policy of retreat and return according to the relative likelihood of an owl attack. Yet another advisor argued strongly for waging outright war upon the stronger owls.

Cloudcolor turned at last to his father, Longlived, and asked his advice. Longlived rejected one by one the earlier war and peace strategies and said that when dealing with a superior foe, deceit spawned in wit was the wisest course to follow. He said, "Pluck out my feathers, abuse me with rough words, smear me with the blood from our dead, and throw me down under this

same tree. Then you go with our survivors to a safe mountain and wait until I provide for the owls' destruction and come to get you."

When Foe-crusher and his owl army returned the next night they could find no crows in the banyan tree. Hearing a feeble cry of a crow under the tree, Foe-crusher discovered Longlived bloodied and near death. The owl king asked the elder crow minister the cause of his terrible condition, and Longlived responded, "My lord, listen. After your warriors had inflicted ruin upon our families, Cloudcolor's counselors encouraged undertaking your destruction. I replied that you and your warriors were too strong and advised Cloudcolor to submit to your rule. Then the other crow advisors said that I was taking sides with the enemy and immediately put me in my present condition."

The owl ministers argued whether or not to kill the wounded elderly crow. One said that a weak enemy, when given a chance, may become strong and harm you. Another owl countered saying it is wrong in war to kill a fugitive even if he is an enemy. "Besides," the second minister continued, "even enemies may be useful when they fall out with each other." Longlived joined the debate by suggesting that it would be best just to throw him into a fire so that he could be reborn an owl and join Foe-crusher as a true ally. Though the first advisor insisted that one's inherited nature is hard to overcome and that Longlived would bring ill to the owls, Foe-crusher decided instead to take the old crow back to the owl stronghold.

Upon arriving at the owls' nests, Foe-crusher ordered that the elderly crow would be permitted to live wherever he chose. Longlived decided that the entrance to the owls' home was the safest place for him to reside. The owls passed by Longlived day after day on their excursions of destruction and were ordered to share with him some meat from their hunting. The old crow regained his strength, grew back his lost feathers, and planned the owls' destruction. One day when the owls were all in their nests asleep, Longlived stuffed rubble in the entrance hole to each nest and then flew off to get Cloudcolor and the other crows. They all returned with fire-sticks and set the rubble-packed owl holes on fire, destroying their enemies.

When commenting upon the success of his strategy, Longlived concluded, "Prowess alone will not bring the supreme desire [defeat of one's enemies] to fruition. Foes that are killed with weapons are not killed, but those that are killed by wit are really killed and never appear again. A weapon kills only a man's body, while wit destroys his tribe, his power, and his renown."

~~~~~

The use of deceit is only one of the many ploys a king may use to defeat his enemies according to the book of fables called the *Panchatantra*. Other war techniques at a king's disposal are conciliation, bribery, sowing dissension among the ranks of the enemy, and outright warring with one's foes. The story of the owls and the crows shows a proper application of deceit as one way to provide kingly protection even when the enemy has superior might.

The image of the king as weak-minded and given over to dangerous passions is one some stories portray. The *Panchatantra* goes so far as to say, "Kings, women, and creeping vines as a rule embrace whatever is beside them." Still, stories that portray various kings as models of compassion and self-sacrifice in providing protection for their people are legion. One such story of this virtuous ideal is that of King Shivi.

A King and a Dove

Once long ago a beautiful dove being pursued by a hawk flew down from the sky and sought the protection of the virtuous King Shivi. Seeing the dove take refuge in his lap, the good king comforted him saying, "Relax little bird, don't be afraid. What have you done that you have become wrapped in the quivering grasp of fear which makes you more dead than alive? Your color, beautiful bird, resembles a wind-blown blue lotus and your eyes are of the tone of a pomegranate or the Ashoka tree. Do not fear, and that is an order! Now that you have sought refuge with me, be advised that no one will even think of harming you, knowing that you have such a powerful protector. If need be, I will for your sake this very day give up my kingdom, or even my life. So, be comforted little dove."

Just then a hawk alighted near the king and said, "This bird you hold has been fated to be my food for today. Therefore, you should not protect him from me, O king. I have pursued this bird with great effort and now have got him. His flesh, blood, marrow, and fat will provide good substance for my welfare and will gratify me greatly. Therefore, O king, do not place yourself between us. I suffer from a terrible thirst, and hunger is gnawing at my bowels. Release this bird and set him free. I am unable to bear the pains of my hunger any longer. I pursued this bird as my prey and you may observe the bruises and cuts on his body my talons and wings have inflicted. Look, O king, and you will see even now that his breath is weak and he is near death, so you should not protect him from me any longer."

Trying a different approach, the hawk continued, "Your power, O king, may extend over your servants, your relatives, and the quarrels that take place between your subjects. In fact your protection and control may extend over all quarters of your kingdom and even over your own senses. Your power, however, does not extend over the sky. Your strength may be demonstrated against foes of your realm and your control may be extended to include them. Still, your rule does not extend to the creatures of the sky, though if it did, you would be as responsible for me and my welfare as for that of the dove."

Hearing these words of the hawk, the king was troubled. Responding to the hawk's claim upon his protection and beneficence, the king responded, "I will order a cow or a deer to be killed and dressed for you today. Please appease your hunger on

61

such food fit for a king. It is my vow never to abandon one who has sought my protection. Observe, O hawk, this little bird huddling in my lap."

The hawk retorted, "O king, I do not eat the flesh of the boar or the cow or any other kinds of fowl. What need have I of such food when it has been ordained that hawks feed on doves? O virtuous king, if you feel such affection for this dove then give me flesh from your own body equal to the weight of this dove."

The king replied, "Thank you for your kindness today in permitting me this alternative solution. I will do as you ask." Having said this, the good king began to cut off his own flesh and weigh it in a balance against the weight of the dove.

The earth began to tremble in response to the king's act. The king continued to cut off flesh from his sides, arms, and thighs and placed it in the scales to balance the weight of the dove. Still, the dove weighed more than the royal flesh. When the king had cut off all his flesh and only remained a skeleton of bones, he ascended the scales himself to give up his very life to balance the scales and keep his promise of protection. Just then, the inhabitants of the three worlds came to behold the righteous king. Celestial and other drums were played by unseen visitors from the sky. King Shivi was bathed in celestial nectar and garlands of heavenly flowers were placed around his neck. The deities and heavenly musicians sang and danced around King Shivi even as they do around the creator Brahma.

The king ascended a heavenly chariot made of gold bedecked with fine jewels as a celestial mansion with gold and jewel columns. Through his act of self-giving protection, the virtuous king then proceeded to heaven.

The tale of King Shivi ends with the admonition, "He who protects those who are devoted to him, those who are attached to him from love and affection, and those who depend upon him, and has mercy on all creatures under his care will acquire great happiness beyond this life." The basic duty of the king is protection. (Not surprisingly, another, allegorical version of this story equates the protected dove with Dharma.) Moreover, kingly protection is to be guided by compassion and self-sacrifice if a king is to be judged virtuous as well as strong.

Buddhist Stories

In the third century B.C. the Buddhist King Ashoka had edicts about righteousness (*dharma*) carved upon large pillars and rocks throughout his kingdom. For example, concerning the religious rituals which the people were accustomed to performing in order to ensure health and welfare, Ashoka wrote (in Rock Edict number nine) that it is far more fruitful to perform Dharma rituals, which consist of treating people properly according to one's relationship to them. Thus, servants should be treated kindly, teachers should be honored, animals should not be killed, and of course priests and ascetics should be protected and nourished. After Ashoka had set such an example, subsequent Buddhist kings felt responsible for promoting social righteousness as well.

The promotion of righteousness was not a luxury for kings however, it was a necessity, as the king in the following story learns from a mountain hermit.

As the King, So the Kingdom

There once was a king who ruled from the city of Banaras with great virtue. He was so eager to please the people that he sought reassurance that he was in fact a good king. He went throughout Banaras inquiring of everyone he met whether or not they considered the king a good ruler.

Everyone answered affirmatively, but the king thought the people might be afraid to be honest with him. He disguised him-

63

self and wandered throughout the area outside the capital, where he was less likely to be recognized. Still, all the people assured him that the king had many merits and no bad points. Then the king, driven on by his need for reassurance, went far north of the city to the foothills of the Himalaya mountains to learn the opinion of the subjects in the most remote area of his rule. There he came upon a mountain hermitage. He approached the hermit, bowed before him with his hands together in respect for the holy man, and sat down in front of him.

Now it happened that the mountain hermit was none other than the Bodhisattva, the Future Buddha. In this particular life the Bodhisattva had been born into a high-class brahman family and had received a formal education as a youth, but upon reaching adulthood had left the comfort and security of city life in order to retreat to the Himalaya region in pursuit of spiritual insight.

The hermit offered the king a ripe fig to eat. When the king tasted the fig he marveled at how sweet it was and asked for an explanation. The hermit said, "The king now rules with justice and impartiality, that is why the fruit is sweet."

The king asked if that meant the fruit would not be as sweet if the king ruled badly. "Precisely," the hermit sage responded, "for when the king is unjust not only wild fruit but also oil, honey, roots, and all other such things in the realm lose their sweetness and flavor."

The king withdrew without revealing his identity and returned to the palace where he began to rule unjustly as an experiment designed to test the sage's words. After a time he returned to the mountain hermitage and was again offered a fig. This time the fig was very bitter and dry, and the king spat it out of his mouth and asked why it tasted so bad. "Evidently the king now rules unjustly," came the reply. "For when a king's justice goes sour the whole kingdom does too," the sage again explained.

The king was convinced of this truth. He revealed his true identity and returned to Banaras more determined than ever to rule with justice.

In the preceding story the legislative and judicial responsibilities of the king are the implied subject matter, but in the following story the king's duty to protect all creatures under his domain comes to the fore. Note that the deer king, like King Shivi in the Hindu story above, is willing to sacrifice his own life to protect a subject.

A Deer King Offers His Life

Once when Brahmadatta was the king of Banaras the Bodhisattva, the Future Buddha, came into existence in the womb of a deer. It was obvious from the moment of his birth that he was a very special deer, for his skin had a golden radiance, his eyes were as round as jewels, his horns were silver colored, his mouth was bright red, his hoofs were as shiny as if they had been lacquered, his tail was like that of a yak, and he was as large as a foal. When the golden deer matured he became the king of a herd of five hundred deer.

There was another golden deer named Branch who similarly was the leader of a large herd in the same forest. The two deer kings were wise and virtuous leaders and all would have been well if the king of Banaras had not been so fond of venison. Nearly every day the king would summon the men of the city from their trades and the men of the country from their farming in order to form a hunting party in quest of a deer from the forest. The people objected to this because they were not able to get their own work done, so they devised a plan. They built a large corral in the royal park and seeded it with grass and provided a water tank. Then they got everyone together to act as beaters, surrounded the forest, and drove the deer into the corral. The two herds of the golden stags were corralled and thus forced to live in the royal park. The king approved of the idea and upon seeing the deer was so struck by the magnificence of the two golden stags that he granted them immunity.

Each day from then on the king or his butcher would go to the corral and shoot arrows into one of the deer until it became so weak from the wounds and exhaustion that it collapsed. There was no escape. The two stags met and planned a way for the deer to avoid this horrible, futile struggle for life. It was determined that each day one deer would be chosen by lot, from each herd on alternate days, and that deer would voluntarily put his head on the chopping block when the king or butcher arrived. This plan worked well until one day the doe that had been chosen by lot from the herd of Branch deer came to Branch begging that another deer be substituted for her on the grounds that she was pregnant and if she were permitted to live there would soon be an extra deer in the herd. Branch refused, saying that he could not ask another deer to take her place. In desperation she took her case to the other golden stag, the Bodhisattva, who sent her away with the assurance that indeed some other deer would take her place.

What the golden stag did was place his own head on the block, much to the astonishment of the butcher. The king was quickly informed and came to the park himself to ask the golden stag why he was volunteering his life when he had been granted immunity. The stag explained about the pregnant doe and said that as king he really could not ask any other deer to volunteer its life, so he himself was ready to die so that the doe might live.

The king was overwhelmed and said that even among humans he had never seen such love and compassion. "I am so pleased with your act," he told the stag, "that I will spare the lives of both you and the doe."

"That is very nice for us," said the stag, "but what of the other deer in the park?" "Very well," said the king, "I will spare their lives as well." "That is very nice for the deer here in the corral, but what about all the others in the forest?" the stag continued. "Very well, I grant them immunity also," the king responded.

The golden stag continued until he had received from the king a promise of immunity for all the creatures of the forests, birds of the air, and fish of the waters. Having in this way converted the king from the violent ways of a hunter to the way of compassion and non-injury to any form of life, which is the first of the five great rules of morality, the golden stag continued to preach to the king about the other virtues; that is, abstaining from stealing, from unlawful sexual intercourse, from lying, and from using intoxicants. "Walk in righteousness," he continued. "Walk in righteousness toward mother and father, sons and daughters, priests and laymen, city and country folk. In this way, when your body breaks up at death, you will go to a blessed heavenly world."

The golden stag remained in the park for a few days teaching righteousness to the king with the ease and skill of a Buddha, and then he departed for the forest to live in peace with his herd. Meanwhile the king followed the wise teaching of the Bodhisattva and was suitably rewarded after death.

The Buddhist tradition considers one of the duties of the king to be that of maintaining peace among the various wandering holy men within his realm. There would be little need for this if all the people who renounce the worldly life and undertake religious vows were indeed holy men, but sometimes they are given to heresy or stubborn bickering. In his role as Protector of Righteousness the king must therefore sometimes intervene in religious matters, as in the following story.

The Day the Sun Did Not Rise

Once when a good king reigned in Banaras two ascetics were traveling through the area and sought overnight lodging in the shed of a certain potter who was in the habit of providing hospitality to wandering holy men. The first ascetic to arrive, who followed the practice of allowing his hair to grow very long and matted, was granted the use of the shed for the night. Before long the second ascetic, a holy man of great power named Narada, arrived and was also granted hospitality, with the permission of the first ascetic.

When night came the potter went home and the two ascetics bedded down on opposite sides of the room. Later in the darkest part of the night Narada wished to go outside for a while, but the matted-haired ascetic had moved and was now lying across the doorway, so that Narada stepped on his hair as he went out. The ascetic awakened furious, scolded Narada, and then began to weep because his hair had been abused.

When Narada returned to the shed he avoided stepping where the ascetic and his hair had been, but because the ascetic had moved, Narada again stepped on his hair. This time the ascetic was even more furious and started calling Narada an "evil ascetic." Narada protested his innocence, but the first ascetic blamed him all the more and finally uttered a curse: "The sun destroys darkness with its thousands of rays; when the sun rises in the morning may your head split in seven pieces."

In self-defense Narada pronounced the same curse upon his rival ascetic, along with the wish that the curse should fall upon whichever of the two was really responsible for the dispute.

As he settled back down for the night Narada used his great mental ability to see into the future and foresaw that the matted-haired ascetic was destined to have his head split at sunrise unless something was done to alter the situation. Out of compassion for his rival, Narada used his great power to keep the sun from rising, thus saving the rival ascetic from destruction.

When the sun failed to rise the people turned to the king for help. The king examined his recent conduct and decided that he had done nothing so wrong as to cause this cosmic standstill. In his wisdom the king guessed that the power of ascetics might be involved, and he was soon led to the potter's shed where Narada explained the situation to the king. In an attempt to mediate the dispute, the king asked Narada what could be done to nullify the curse. The curse could be broken if the ascetic apologized,

Narada replied. The king turned to the matted-hair ascetic and asked him to apologize, but the stubborn man refused. After more futile attempts with words, the king became desperate enough to order his soldiers to force the ascetic to bow before Narada, as if for forgiveness.

Although this was hardly a sincere apology, Narada forgave the ascetic and asked the king to have the ascetic put in a lake up to his neck in water, with a large ball of clay on top of his head. When this was done Narada allowed the sun to rise and as its first light fell across the lake the clay ball split into seven pieces, but the ascetic submerged himself and was not hurt. In this way peace was restored by the king and all the people were able to return to work.

⁓

The Chronicles of the Island of Sri Lanka (Ceylon) record that the Buddhist kings there often took their role as Protector of Righteousness so seriously that they intervened in disputes among religious leaders, as did the king in the preceding story. These Sri Lankan kings supported some monasteries while holding others suspect of heresy, and one king went so far as to destroy the most important monastery on the island when his chaplain convinced him it promulgated heretical ideas (*Mahavamsa*, Ch. 37). More typical, however, was the practice of royal intervention in cases involving flagrant abuse of clerical privileges. There were usually some scoundrels ready to put on the guise of spirituality, and it fell to the king to bring them to justice.

TEACHER / PRIEST
Hindu Stories

The *Laws of Manu* (10.75, 83) relates the basic duties of the brahmans or priests as comprising: studying and teaching the sacred traditions and texts, performing private and public sacrifices for worldly harmony and personal needs of the people, and refraining from vocations such as farming or those requiring manual labor which would lower the prestige of their social rank. The brahmans are viewed as the intercessors between humans and the divine world, and consequently as having fearful power as well as the world's future in their hands. The Epic tale which follows shows both the high status of the brahmans as well as the reciprocal support which exists between kings and priests. Most important of all, the priest is pictured here as preserver and conveyor of the sacred traditions which he transmits in his role as a storyteller.

The Brahman and the Demons

Various demons continually disturbed the sacrifices of the renowned sage Vishvamitra. Deeply concerned, the forest priest went quickly to the court of King Dasharatha to secure protection. Seeing the venerable sage enter his audience hall, the king said, "My birth is blessed with good fruits and my life made valuable simply by observing your presence in my court. The viewing of your holy form turns the darkest night into brightest day. . . . Say what it is you would have me do and it will be done."

The sage explained to the king that, as was his priestly duty, he performed his devotional rites every day. However, the forests surrounding his hermitage were filled with demons bent upon disrupting the holy sacrifices. Daily the demons would come spreading bloody meat and entrails upon the sacred alter, voiding hours of preparation for this most holy of priestly rituals. Vishvamitra explained that he had come to ask the king's protection. The king asked what he could do, and the priest responded that the king's sons Rama and Lakshman should accompany the sage back to his forest retreat. The king protested that Rama was too young and no match for the might of demons. The king pleaded, "Please show pity on my dear child and release me from this unhappy fate. . . . For I venerate you as a god and must obey your command." The king's pleas were of no avail since his kingly duty demanded that he guarantee protection to all priests and people in his realm.

Dawn broke over the sage Vishvamitra setting off toward his forest abode with young Rama and Lakshman cheerfully at his side. As they stopped at one hermitage and then the next, Vishvamitra performed his various priestly rites, explaining to the young warriors the history of his sacred duties and telling stories of the gods and men who had occupied the holy sites. Early on the second day of their journey, the three travelers arrived at the edge of a dark forest. Rama asked why the forest appeared so forbidding. Vishvamitra explained that the demoness Tadaka lived in the dark woods and then told the story of how a beautiful maiden had become a mad demoness by the curse of a brahman priest. He warned that Tadaka still roamed the dreary forest ruining the sacrifices of the priests within.

Rama strung his warrior's bow and entered the forest to engage Tadaka in combat and rid the forest sages of their perturbance. Plucking his bow's sounding string, Rama awakened Tadaka from her slumber. The angry demoness arose to fight the young warrior and assailed him with all her evil might. Though Tadaka showered them with stones, Rama and Lakshman fired arrow after arrow, severing the demoness's hands, nose, and ears. Screeching in tumultuous rage, Tadaka became invisible and increased her rain of stones. Rama quickly unleashed an arrow in the direction of the sound of Tadaka's roar, and the deadly shaft pierced

Tadaka's bowels and ended her evil life. Freed from Tadaka's malicious interference, the priestly sages of the dark forest renewed their sacrifices which sustain the earth and the heavens.

As a gift for the young warriors, Vishvamitra taught Rama and Lakshman the use of powerful weapons and divine spells to increase their princely might. As they journeyed together, the venerable sage taught the young princes by telling them stories about the origin of places, gods, and people which devoted warriors should know. When at last they reached the hermitage where Vishvamitra usually performed his religious observances, the hermits who lived there came and each washed the sage's feet and offered him food and a place to rest.

Early the next morning Vishvamitra began the rite of purification in preparation for the daily sacrifice. Reciting sacred texts, the sage sanctified the holy fire. Just then, a roar introduced the onslaught of two grotesque demons. Raining down blood to spoil the sacrifice, the demons quickly found themselves engaged in battle with Rama and Lakshman. One arrow from Rama's quiver knocked one demon senseless as it carried him to a lake far from the forest of Vishvamitra's hermitage. A second arrow split the other demon's stomach, ending his demonic intrusions. Then Rama and Lakshman destroyed, one by one, the remaining demons in the forest, liberating the forest sages from demonic distractions. The priests within the forest sent up a cheer for the protectors of their sacred rites. The sacrifices which keep the world harmonious could once again be performed.

In spite of the exalted role of the priest which Vishvamitra provides, many stories show the brahmans capable of utilizing their near-divine powers destructively to curse and harm those who have offended them. The following episode from the epic tradition of the *Mahabharata* reveals the awesome and irrevocable might of the curse of a priest.

73

The Curse of a Brahman

The great King Parikshit loved hunting. Once while searching for game he shot and wounded a deer which took him on a prolonged chase deep into a strange forest. After tracking the wounded deer for many hours and having become tired and thirsty from the search, the king came upon a hermitage in a clearing in the woods. Seeing an ascetic priest sitting on the ground near his cows, the king approached the sage and said, "Brahman, I am King Parikshit and I am tracking a deer which I have wounded. Have you seen that deer?" The brahman sat in silence due to a vow he had taken earlier. The king asked again for the brahman to speak and again received no reply. Tired, frustrated, and now angry, King Parikshit took a dead snake by the end of his bow and placed the serpent around the ascetic's neck. When the brahman bore this insult in silence, the king felt his anger subside and he gave up his search for the wounded deer and returned home empty-handed.

As the brahman's son was on the road home that day, one of his friends teased him about his father's disgrace—sitting with a serpent around his neck. Embarrassed, the son asked what had caused his father's disgrace. When he was told the story of how King Parikshit had come to place the snake around his father's shoulders, the son angrily said, "That wretched king who placed a dead snake upon the shoulders of my frail, old parent shall be killed in seven days by the king of serpents, Takshaka." Hurrying home, the son approached his father who still had the dead snake around his neck and told him of the curse of death he had pronounced.

The old brahman responded, "Son, I am not pleased with you. Ascetics should not behave this way. We live under the rule of King Parikshit and he protects all priests under his care. He did not know that I had taken a vow of silence and thus acted as he understood the situation. The king did not deserve your curse and you acted hastily. I will send a messenger and try to ward off the king's demise." The son responded, "Father, whether I acted rashly or not, you know that the curse of a brahman is never thwarted."

When King Parikshit learned of the curse against his life from the old brahman's messenger, he was both saddened about his improper treatment of the old priest and worried about his own welfare. After counsel from his advisors, Parikshit built a platform upon posts so that neither Takshaka nor his serpent helpers could approach the king unobserved. Then the king built dwelling quarters upon the platform.

As the fateful week drew to a close, Takshaka sent several of his servants disguised as ascetics to offer King Parikshit some water, nuts, and fruit. The king permitted the ascetics to ascend his platform and after receiving the gifts, bade the ascetics farewell. After the ascetics had departed the king invited his ministers to join him in eating the fruits the ascetics had given him. Just as King Parikshit was about to bite into his fruit, an ugly black and copper-colored insect came out of the fruit. The king said, "The sun is setting on the seventh day, and I am not afraid of Takshaka's poison. Therefore, assume your true form Takshaka and fulfill the brahman's curse."

Just then, the insect was transformed into a large serpent and Takshaka coiled himself around the neck of King Parikshit. Emitting a tremendous roar, Takshaka ended the life of King Parikshit with a deadly bite.

Even though the brahman who had been wronged did not desire King Parikshit's death, "the curse of a brahman is never thwarted," the epic tale proclaims. The priests who claim to rank highest among humans and who, as ascetics, should be above human emotions such as anger, often are pictured to be like the son of the offended sage. At his best, the priest uses his learning and power to nourish and enrich those about him, but, as often as not, the Indian stories of priests provide images of angry or self-centered men whose curse is to be feared and whose lives are hardly models for virtuous conduct.

Buddhist Stories

Gautama Buddha spent the last forty-five years of his life traveling about northern India teaching. He is revered as the Enlightened One (the Buddha) primarily, but he is also revered as the great teacher. Buddhists believe that from time to time a Buddha appears in the world and teaches eternal Truth (*dharma*), but as time passes a particular Buddha's teachings are gradually forgotten, and eventually there is need for a new Buddha. Each new Buddha when he becomes enlightened and begins to teach *Dharma* is said to be again "setting the dharma-wheel in motion." Here in brief is the story Gautama tells of setting the wheel in motion.

Buddha Sets the Wheel in Motion

Monks, after I had struggled so long and hard for enlightenment and finally achieved it, I thought to myself, "This Dharma which I have won is very profound, difficult to understand, advanced, and intelligible only to those of great learning. But most people are attached to sensual pleasures and cannot comprehend such a Dharma. Therefore, if I were to try to teach this Dharma to them, I would just wear myself out to no avail."

Then the god Brahma read my mind from heaven and he worried that the world would be lost if the Buddha decided not to teach Dharma. So, monks, as quickly as a strong man can stretch out his arm, the god Brahma disappeared from heaven and reappeared on earth next to me. He arranged his robes and approached me reverently, saying, "Venerable sir, let the Lord teach Dharma. Let the Accomplished One teach Dharma. There are some people in the world who are close enough to the truth to be able to benefit from your teaching."

Then, monks, I surveyed the whole world with the supernatural third eye of a Buddha, and I saw that there were some people with only a little dust in their eyes. It occurred to me that just as in a lotus pond, some lotuses never rise above the water, some get just to the top but others rise above the water and their blue, red, or white blossoms are not spoiled by the dirty water, so there are some persons who can rise above the stains of the world with the help of Dharma teaching.

Brahma, being pleased with my decision to teach, paid reverence to me and instantaneously returned to his heaven. I then considered whom I should instruct first. I thought of my two former yoga teachers, but with my Buddha eye I realized that they had already died. So I decided to teach the five ascetics who were my companions while I practiced severe asceticism. By means of my Dharma eye I discerned that they were staying in the park at Banaras, so I began to journey there.

When the five ascetics saw me coming they said to themselves, "Friends, let us shun this Gautama, for he has fallen away from his ascetic practices. He now eats good meals. Do not rise to greet him nor take his robe." But when I got close enough for them to see my transformed countenance, they abandoned their haughtiness and received me hospitably, saying, "Welcome, friend Gautama." I explained to them, "Do not address an Enlightened One by his personal name or by the word *friend*. Listen to me, monks, I will teach you Dharma as a saint, a fully enlightened Buddha."

〜〜〜

The virtue of always telling the truth is an important one for teachers in the Buddhist tradition. The virtue of doing what the master asks is just as important for students, but the following story provides an example of how such virtues may be set aside when the situation warrants.

A Teacher's Tricky Test

Once when Brahmadatta was the king of Banaras the Bodhisattva was born into a brahman family in Banaras. When he matured he went off to study under a renowned teacher and was at the head of a class of five hundred. After he had studied there for some time the teacher decided to marry his daughter to whichever student was the most virtuous. To test them he announced that the student who brought him the most stolen cloth and jewels for his daughter's dowry could have her hand in marriage.

The students studied by day and stole by night, as the contest proceeded, until the teacher had a large pile of stolen goods from each of them except the Bodhisattva. When the teacher asked the Bodhisattva why he had not yet brought anything taken in secret, the youth replied that there was no such thing as secrecy. He composed a verse of poetry for the master making the point that no sinful act is ever totally "in secret" for the spirits of the woods may see the act committed, and, at any rate, the criminal himself will be his own witness.

The master called the students together and explained that the test was a trick to see which was the most virtuous. He gave his daughter in marriage to the Bodhisattva and made the other students return the stolen goods.

Later Indian Buddhism (the Mahayana school) emphasized the fact that the Buddha teaches by "skillful means," that is, by cleverly chosen devices which may from one point of view be deceptions but from another point of view are more than justified because they lead the hearers toward eternal Truth. The most famous passage on "skillful means" in Buddhist literature is the following allegory from one of the most popular of all Mahayana Buddhist texts, *The Lotus of the True Law*.

78

How the Clever Father Saved His Sons

Once there was a rich man who lived in a three-storied house made of wood and thatch. The house was old, dilapidated, and a firetrap. One day as the man came out of the house he noticed to his horror that the roof of the house was ablaze and the fire was spreading very quickly. He knew he must act fast to save his many sons who were playing in various parts of the house, unaware of the danger.

His first thought was to dash into the house and gather up the children in his arms, but then he realized that the boys would think he was playing a game and run from him and hide. So he decided to call to them to come out quickly. He called, "Fire! Fire! Boys, come out quickly, the house is burning down!" But this did not work. The boys just did not seem to understand the gravity of the situation and they went right on playing.

The father then realized that he must employ some skillful means to entice them out of the house. Thinking quickly, he called out to them, "Boys, come on out. I have some presents for you." Since he knew that his boys desired different things, he added, "I have deer carts, goat carts and bullock carts. Come on out quickly and I will give each of you whatever cart you wish." With happy cries of "Race you out," all the boys came rushing out of the burning house, eager for the carts.

Boys being the way boys are, once they were out of the burning house, they asked their father where the carts were that he promised. In his joy at saving his sons, the father decided to get them the best carts money could buy. He bought each of them a deluxe customized bullock cart with inlaid jewels, pretty sounding bells, and beautiful trim, complete with bullocks to pull them. The boys climbed on the carts and proudly drove them about in great excitement.

When the Buddha had finished telling this story to his disciple Sariputra, he asked him if the father in the story was guilty of lying. Sariputra responded that in no way should the use of skillful means for a higher purpose be labeled "lying," for even if the father had not gone out and bought carts for the boys he still would not be blamable for promising them carts. The Buddha then explained the allegory to Sariputra. The three stories of the house represent the three levels of the universe. The fire in the house represents the misery which the world suffers. The Buddha is like a father who sees the danger his children are in. But merely calling warnings to them is not enough, so he uses skillful means such as teaching them that there are three kinds of "vehicles" or spiritual paths which they can follow (the paths of the disciple, of the private Buddha, and of the teaching Buddha). Eventually, when they are ready to understand better, he explains that the only real vehicle (according to this Buddhist text) is that of the compassionate teaching Buddha.

ASCETIC
Hindu Stories

Asceticism is a bit difficult to understand in those cultures where physical pleasures and pride in appearance are so highly regarded. While the Indian religious and cultural traditions encourage worldly and economic success as well as the enjoyment of sensual pleasures, it is the ascetic's life which is claimed to be the highest and final life-stage for a person who would prepare for a more permanent existence, beyond the reach of death. The options for worldly attachment and detachment are stated quite clearly in the *Matsya Purana* (3.38-40) which says, "The 88,000 sages who desired offspring went south and obtained graves, but the 88,000 sages who did not desire offspring went north and obtained immortality."

Just as a woman's attraction is the most feared of all worldly enticements, passion is the one emotion to be quelled if the ascetic is to gain any level of success. Of all the forms of attachment to the world, it is the emotional bond between persons of the opposite sex that most easily deters renunciation of the world. In the story which follows, even an accomplished ascetic falls to passion personified as Kama, the Indian Cupid.

The Monkey-Faced Suitor

The renowned sage Narada once decided to do austere penances in order to control all of his emotions and desires. Upon seating himself in the conducive setting of a great hermitage, Narada began his yogic practice. He sat for days in silence, controlling his breath and keeping his mind free of impure thoughts. The very throne of Indra, lord of the gods, became agitated by the heat generated by Narada's austerities. Indra became worried that he might lose his lordship to this mere mortal unless he could persuade Narada to abandon his penance. Indra sent for Kama, the god of love. Explaining to Kama his predicament, Indra said, "O friend of great prowess . . . , render me your assistance. Narada, the sage, is performing a penance in the Himalaya mountain, directing his mind towards the lord of the universe. . . . I now fear lest he should beg of Brahma, the lord of creation, my kingdom. You must go there now and hinder his penance."

Kama went to the hermitage of Narada with his lovely wife Rati and began his many illusory tricks, such as causing spring to come early with its sweet flowers and fragrances. But no matter which of the arts of love Kama tried, Narada remained unmoved in meditation. Kama left Narada's hermitage seeming to have lost the battle with this ideal sage.

Realizing his penance to be complete and thinking he had thoroughly overcome love's enticements, Narada ceased his penances and left the hermitage. Puffed up by the pride of his ascetic achievements, Narada set off to the heaven of Shiva [the god of ascetic renown] to brag of his newly acquired achievements. Shiva received him with praise for his defeat of Kama. Being encouraged, Narada then went to the lord of creation, Brahma, and to Vishnu, the supreme god of protection and mercy, and continued his boasting about his conquest of passion. Concerned at the pridefulness of the sage who thought himself to be above such human emotions, the gods planned a test of Narada's ascetic calm.

A city more beautiful than heaven itself was placed in Narada's path as he made his way back to earth from his heavenly sojourn. The king who lived in this city was preparing to hold a husband-choosing ceremony for his daughter Shrimati in which she would pick her own husband. As Narada approached the palace of the king, the king's daughter came to wait upon the venerable sage.

Narada was struck dumb by the princess's beauty. When he learned that the king was holding a husband-choosing ceremony for the beautiful princess, Narada, overcome by passionate longings, decided that he must be the one chosen by the girl.

Narada ran back to Vishnu's heavenly abode and begged the handsome god to bestow his good looks upon him to secure Narada's chances of being chosen by the pretty maiden. Narada said, "O Lord, give me your form. I am your servant and favorite. Give me your beautiful form so that the princess Srimati may choose me." Vishnu responded, "O sage, you can go to the place where you wish. I shall do what is beneficial for you just as a physician does what is good for his patients." Thereupon, Vishnu blessed the sage with his godly form and the face of Hari [another name of Vishnu which means both "delightful or charming" and "monkey"]. Thus, from a play on words, the sage Narada set off to the husband-choosing ceremony with the body of a god and the face of a monkey.

Narada hurried back to the palace of the king to attend the husband-choosing ceremony. In the great hall of the palace where the ceremony was to take place, there were assembled scores of princes all anxious to be chosen by the beautiful Shrimati. Not knowing his actual appearance, Narada thought, "She will choose only me since I am in Vishnu's form." Several of those attending the ceremony mocked Narada's appearance and laughed at his delusive pride. Just then, the princess came out of her chambers and began to walk down the line of anxious suitors with a garland of flowers to bedeck her choice. When she came to Narada she was infuriated at the affront of a monkey-faced man believing he had a chance to be chosen. Shrimati ran from the ceremonial hall without choosing a husband.

Narada was perplexed at the princess's response to his countenance until he was told by two divine attendants, "O sage Narada, being deluded by love, you are desirous of getting her. Your effort is in vain. You see, your face is as despicable as that of a monkey."

While the story of Narada may well provide an image of an ascetic who failed in his attempt to become detached from transitory enticements, the ascetic in India is not without a model. The god Shiva demonstrates his supreme asceticism in the following story.

The Destruction of Love

Indra, the lord of the gods, was at his wit's end. The demon Taraka roamed about heaven and earth wreaking destruction, and no mortal or god could defeat him. Taraka had once been granted the boon of dying only at the hands of a son of the ascetic and destructive god Shiva, and Shiva was firmly seated in meditation which was to continue for years to come. The question Indra struggled with was how Shiva might be awakened from his yogic trance and be encouraged to sport with his spouse

84

Parvati in order to father a son who could relieve the world from the oppressive Taraka.

Indra decided that only the passion-arousing enticements issuing from Kama, the god of love, could break Shiva's ascetic concentration. Love's embodiment, Kama, was begged by Indra to assist the whole world in its dire need. Kama assented and set off for the forest where Shiva was engaged in fasting and yogic meditation.

Upon arriving at Shiva's hermitage, Kama set in motion the snares of passion for which he was famous. Spring was activated with its soft winds carrying fresh fragrances. The sweet-smelling mango blossoms sent forth their enchanting aromas. The Ashoka trees sparkled with their bright flowers of springtime. Bees hovered above the water lilies causing love to rise in the minds of all within view. The mating coos of the doves heightened feelings of affection in the hearts of all living things. These lurings of spring agitated even the most resolute of forest ascetics.

Through all Kama's efforts, Shiva sat unperturbed and calm, untouched by the god of love. Just then, the maiden Parvati came with two attendants to bring flowers for Shiva's worship. Shiva came out of his concentrated state for a short while to receive Parvati's display of devotion. Seeing his chance, Kama discharged his flowery arrows at the awakened Shiva. Shiva then began to notice the lovely limbs of the graceful Parvati. He began to describe her beauty in words used by lovers and poets.

Moved by Kama's enticements and Parvati's beauty, Shiva said, "I feel great pleasure just looking at Parvati. How much greater the joy would be if I would embrace her."

Immediately upon thinking these lustful thoughts Shiva became detached again and observed, "Though I am lord of all ascetics, I have been perturbed by Kama. . . . How is it that obstacles have cropped up while I am performing great penances? Who can be that wicked person who has made my mind greatly perturbed?" Looking around his hermitage, Shiva saw Kama hiding among the trees and about to discharge another flower arrow. Instantaneous anger was aroused in Shiva, and the flower arrow of Kama struck the ascetic lord to no avail. Kama dropped his bow and trembled with fright. A bright flame issued forth from the third eye located in the forehead of Shiva and, resembling the fire of the world's dissolution, shot forth into the sky. When that fire returned to earth it rolled over the earth reducing Kama and his enticements to a pile of ashes. The enticements of the god of love had failed finally to prevail over Shiva, the lord of all ascetics.

Buddhist Stories

Buddhism grew from ascetic soil in northern India in the sixth century B.C. Gautama practiced severe asceticism for a while, as the first story describes, and later softened his position toward that of a "middle path." But even the way of the middle path seems rather ascetic from the point of view of an overfed, indulgent Western society. Gautama's middle path prescribed only one full meal a day, no food after lunchtime, few hours of sleep, no sexual contact, and so on. Buddhist monks and nuns have followed these rules through the centuries and found that the spiritual advantages offset the loss in bodily gratification.

The following story was told by Gautama Buddha to a monk of the Jain religious tradition, which advocates strict ascetic practices as a means to spiritual salvation.

Buddha Finds a Middle Path

Back in the days when I was a Bodhisattva trying various paths toward enlightenment it occurred to me to undertake an absolute fast. But while I was contemplating this some angels came to me and asked me not to abstain totally from food and drink. If I did, they would feed me through my pores, they assured me.

So I undertook a slightly less severe fast instead. For many days I ingested only a few drops of soup each day, and I became very emaciated. My arms and legs became like withered vines; my buttocks shrivelled up, my backbone and ribs protruded greatly, and my scalp shrank. When I sought to touch my stomach, I reached my backbone, and vice versa. I often fell down while attempting to urinate or defecate. When I stroked my arms the hair would come out because the roots were rotting. My skin tone changed so much that people remarked that I was black or dark brown complexioned.

Then I realized that severe fasting was not getting me any closer to enlightenment, so I tried to think of some other approach. I remembered that as a child I had entered into a blissful state of wakeful meditation under a tree while my father was ploughing. With that experience in mind I ate food again, in moderation, and began the practice of meditation which led to my enlightenment.

⟿

The preceding story makes the point that ascetic practices alone, no matter how severe, will not lead to higher spiritual knowledge. The Buddhist middle path recommends moderation concerning the bodily needs, and most monks have not been overly ascetic. Yet there is another type of asceticism, which involves withdrawing from worldly responsibilities in order to concentrate upon spiritual development. This latter dimension of asceticism is highly valued in the Buddhist tradition, as the following story reveals.

The Man Who Wouldn't Be King

Once when Brahmadatta was king of Banaras the Bodhisattva came into existence in the womb of a brahman woman whose husband was the king's chaplain. A son was born to the king on the same day, and the two boys were raised together and even dressed alike. They were sent off to school together and later as adults at court remained great friends.

Eventually the prince became king and the chaplain's son began to think seriously about his own career. He guessed that sooner or later his close friend, the king, would appoint him to the high position of king's chaplain, which would make him the most honored priest in the land. But he was more interested in spiritual development than honor at court, so with his parents' permission he left the court and the city behind and journeyed north to the Himalaya mountains. There he built a hermit's hut and enjoyed dwelling in meditational states of mind.

Meanwhile the king missed his old friend and was informed that he had gone to meditate in the mountains. The king told a messenger, "Go and bring my friend back and I will give him the office of king's chaplain." The messenger found the hermit meditating, motionless like a golden statue, in front of the hermitage. "Reverend Sir," the messenger said, "the king desires you to return to court as king's chaplain."

To the surprise of the messenger the Bodhisattva refused, saying he would not return to be the king's chaplain or even to be the king of all India. A wise man would no more take up again the [worldly] defilements [kilesa-] he had left behind than the ordinary man would again swallow phlegm [khelasa-] he had spit out, he explained. He then recited some verses of poetry which stated that no throne could tempt him away from his spiritual life and that it is better to be a homeless beggar than a king, given all the temptations to power and oppression that go with the office.

The messenger paid respect to the holy man and returned to report to the king.

88

The stories in this chapter exhibit again the great extent to which traditional India's roles and values can be communicated in story form. In both the Buddhist and Hindu traditions the stories emphasize the great responsibility the king has for the protection of the people, animals, and land under his rule. The king should be willing to substitute his own life for that of a subject who has turned to him for protection, according to the model provided in several of the stories. Hindu stories put more emphasis upon the king's duty to protect his subjects with might and cunning, while the Buddhist stories stress the way the whole domain responds automatically to the righteousness or unrighteousness of the ruler. Compassion is a quality in kings which both Hindu and Buddhist stories advance. The Buddhist stories also described the model king as one who intervenes when necessary in quarrels which arise among ascetics.

Both Hinduism and Buddhism venerated the teacher/priest, but here there is often more diversity than in stories of the kings. Hindu stories usually depict a sage as a learned brahman who instructs people of all castes in the knowledge of traditional and supernatural matters, while piously continuing the sacrifices which sustain the world. He gains his status by his birth into a brahman family, which brings him great respect. However, the brahman's power may on occasion be turned against others in anger, which gives rise to a fearsome image of the brahman. The Buddhist stories on the other hand provide a model of the teacher-monk as a man who, having left family or worldly life behind in order to gain wisdom, selflessly desires to share it with others. Such a teacher may find it necessary to practice what might seem to be deceptions, according to some schools of Buddhism, but in his higher understanding the seeming deceptions are instruments of invaluable instruction.

In both the Hindu and Buddhist stories the teacher or priest is a person of great spiritual knowledge that has typically been gained by long hours of meditation and study, and the final section of the chapter presented stories about Hindus and Buddhists engaged in the ascetic practices in hope of gaining spiritual knowledge and power. In both traditions it is taken for granted that ascetics must remain strictly celibate, and many stories tell of the sensual temptations that ascetics have faced, to their detriment or their credit. Many Hindu stories emphasize the psychic and physical powers that come from prolonged periods of austerities. Although the Buddhists also believed that such powers resulted from meditational practices, they were skeptical of any meditator who made it his goal to gain psychic powers rather than wisdom. The emphasis in the Buddhist stories is upon finding a middle path between indulgence and self-torture, but with some idealization of the monastic life.

The stories in the first two chapters present some negative images of and some positive models for the roles Hindus and Buddhists play in families and in the larger society. We have found that these images and models *imply* religious doctrine and practice. We now turn to stories that deal more directly with religious values.

3
Lay Values

It is a bit artificial to call some Indian religious values and demands "lay" and others "monastic" for both groups share many religious sanctions and requirements. For example, the "Universal" Hindu duties (*dharmas*) number five and are applicable to every member of the top three classes regardless of social station or occupation. These five duties are: (1) to avoid causing injury to living creatures (*ahimsa*), (2) to abstain from stealing, (3) to abstain from lying, (4) to engage only in proper sexual behavior, and (5) to remain aloof from material attachments (for Hindus) or to abstain from intoxicants (for Buddhists). Nonetheless, it is also the case that what is required of a person changes according to the class level into which he is born or to his life-stage. For example, a householder is not only permitted the necessary sexual activity which his obligation to produce sons implies, but is also encouraged to enjoy sex for pleasure alone as the householder's duty of love (*kama*) suggests. When that same person, however, takes the vows of the forest dweller or ascetic upon himself, strict chastity is required. Likewise, there are real distinctions made in India between the religious duties of the laity and those of the individual or communal "world-renouncer," as is implicit in some of the stories of the previous chapters.

Stories have been included in this chapter which will permit the distinctively Hindu or Buddhist emphases to surface, while allowing areas of agreements also to remain.

COURAGE
Hindu Stories

While the orthodox Hindu stand regarding killing is that of *ahimsa* or non-injury to any living creature, the religious duty of the warrior (and king) often came into conflict with that general moral requirement. Since the duty of the warrior is to protect by his might the people under his king's rule, killing of others in the line of duty is not only required but praised. In the story which follows, a young warrior's courage is immortalized by his ferocious, self-neglecting charge into an enemy formation. Here it is valor and death-dealing courage rather than non-injury which are extolled.

The Warrior's Death

On the twelfth day of the great battle between the two great clans of the Bharata family, the evil forces of Duryodhana were led into battle by the mighty archer Drona. Deploying his army in a circle formation, Drona attacked Yudhishthira's army which was weakened by the absence of its strongest warrior, Arjuna, who was fighting elsewhere that day. Again and again Yudhishthira's army tried to break through the circle of bowmen who protected Drona, but each thrust proved costlier than the previous one. Meanwhile, Drona inflicted heavy casualties and threatened to overrun those who would protect Yudhishthira from capture.

Just as it appeared that all was lost, Arjuna's son Abhimanyu came forward and said, "I will go forward and break the band of archers who protect Drona. My father has taught me how to do this. It is clear, however, that if anything goes wrong I will not be able to get away."

King Yudhishthira responded, "Go forward, best of warriors, and make a passage for us. We shall all follow you into the breach and help you turn back the enemy."

Abhimanyu set out in his chariot. Like a shaft of lightning piercing a dark sky, he charged furiously into the outer line of Drona's circle defense. Shooting arrows and thrusting with his sword at the same time, Abhimanyu broke through the first line of Drona's archers. The brave warrior continued his charge as he struck down enemy soldiers mounted on elephants and chariots. The warriors around the enemy king Duryodhana became confused by Abhimanyu's furious rush, and the angry king called upon all in the inner circle of defense to concentrate their force upon this young warrior.

One after another of the gallant warriors of Drona encountered Abhimanyu in hand-to-hand combat, and each one was killed or left dying. So frightening was the charge of Abhimanyu that some of Drona's warriors began to flee. It appeared that Abhimanyu had broken the circle-defense. As he approached Drona's chariot, he was attacked by Drona's son and struck by sixty arrows. Returning his antagonist's punishment, Abhimanyu wounded Drona's son with dozens of arrows. At that point, the master of archers, Drona himself, entered the fight. Discharging over one hundred arrows, Drona dealt a near deathblow to Abhimanyu from which none of the young warrior's allies could save him. Weakened from his wounds and deprived of his bow and chariot by the skillful shots of his opponents, Abhimanyu charged on foot toward Drona's chariot. Abhimanyu was finally felled by the blow of a war club to his head, but not before he had stopped the seemingly inexorable onslaught of Drona's circle formation.

The sage Vyasa consoled King Yudhishthira, on whose behalf young Abhimanyu had fought and died, by saying, "Great king, you have much wisdom and you know that you should not be overcome by such a misfortune. This brave young warrior [Abhimanyu] who killed many enemy soldiers will attain heaven." In other words, in spite of the general moral requirement of non-injury, killing in the line of duty (when done courageously and according to the laws of war) can itself provide the reward of heaven. It seems obvious, therefore, that courage and valor are more desirable traits for the lay warrior than would be a refusal to kill. (See Krishna's instructions to Arjuna in chapter two of the *Bhagavad Gita*.)

In the following story, the goddess (whom we will call Devi though she was also known by other names) is described and glorified in a divinized version of the values of courage, valor, and destructive might such as Abhimanyu displayed in the preceding story.

The Goddess Who Drank Blood

The gods had been defeated in a one-hundred-year war by the demons (*asuras*), and the throne of Indra, the lord of the gods, had been taken by Mahishasura, the lord of demons. The gods went to the unsurpassable divinities Vishnu and Shiva and begged for their help. Out of the anger of Shiva and Vishnu there arose a great light which took bodily form, and the form was that of a magnificent and radiant goddess who bore the names Durga, Kali, Chandika, and Devi. Each of the assembled gods gave to this goddess his own weapon. The Wind gave his quiver of arrows, Indra gave a bolt of lightning, etc.

Endowed with the best virtues and powers of all the gods, Devi let out a deep-throated roar which terrified all the unrighteous and sounded to them like the roar of death itself. All the worlds shook, the earth quaked, and the mountains trembled at the sound she emitted. The demon Mahishasura and his demon allies rushed immediately to the place of Devi's roar and found the goddess seated upon her lion waiting for them to engage her in battle.

One by one Mahishasura's prized warriors went out to challenge the goddess in combat and one by one they were killed. No matter what weapon a demon used, Devi's might was greater. Some demons were decapitated, others had their limbs unceremoniously removed, while still others were divided in half by her broad sword. The battlefield ran knee-deep with the blood of the demons and their mounts, and it seemed that no force could stem the onslaught of Devi's carnage.

Seeing his army decimated by the now roaring goddess, Mahishasura sent out his most trusted general to do battle with her. The demon general showered a rain of arrows upon the goddess, but she playfully cut all the arrow shafts into small pieces. Then she advanced to engage the demon face to face and immediately killed his horse and driver. The demon retaliated with a blow from his mighty sword, only to have his weapon shatter into pieces upon impact with the goddess's arm. With one blow from her mighty arm, Devi killed the demon general, leaving Mahishasura alone.

Mahishasura assumed his terrible buffalo form, and charged Devi's army, destroying many soldiers as he went. With his horns he cut open some warriors, with his tail he knocked others unconscious, and with his hooves he disembodied still others. Finally, the demon lord in buffalo form charged the lion upon which Devi sat. As he charged, the buffalo-demon tossed mountains aside with his horns and dug valleys in the earth with his hooves. Seeing the ominous charge of the buffalo form of Mahishasura, Devi produced a noose by which she caught the charg-

ing buffalo and threw it to the ground. Just as she was about to pierce the buffalo with her spear, the demon gave up his buffalo disguise and adopted that of a lion. As Devi decapitated the lion form of Mahishasura, he assumed a human form. And as Devi destroyed his human guise, Mahishasura again entered the buffalo form. Before he could do any more damage or assume yet another form, Devi cut off the demon's head while the whole demon army let out a mournful cry. The demon which had terrorized the heavens and the earth was now dead, and the goddess hungrily drank the blood of the dead demons which covered the battlefield.

Buddhist Stories

The Buddhists were one of several sectarian movements centered around the Ganges River, which separated from the Hindu mainstream in the sixth and fifth centuries B.C. Most of these groups were especially concerned with the teaching of non-violence. One group had reached a novel compromise between the desire to sustain life and the desire to avoid killing humans or animals; they collectively killed one elephant a year and lived on its dried flesh. In this way each member of the group accumulated only the relatively small amount of bad karma which accrues from being partly responsible for only one act of violence per year. Most of the other sects, including the Buddhists, refused to compromise their non-violent stance and undertook to avoid killing even worms and mosquitoes. It was impossible for farmers and most lay people to practice non-violence to such an extent, however, so it was thought necessary to take on the homeless life if one wished to follow the teaching completely. As homeless ascetics, the practitioners of non-violence were freed of the killing involved in plowing, fishing, or hunting, and many took further precautions such as straining small animals out of their drinking water and avoiding walking when rains had brought worms to the earth's surface.

Their non-violent stance made the Buddhists shun the traditional values of courage in battle. Instead they idealized people who had the courage to resist traditional forms of killing. The first of the following stories teaches that even animals should not be killed. The second is typical of the many Buddhist stories about men who had the courage *not* to bear arms in the face of danger.

The Goat Who Laughed and Cried

Once when Brahmadatta was king of Banaras a certain brahman, who was very learned in the scriptures and a famous teacher, decided to perform the ritual appropriate for honoring his ancestors. This ritual centers upon the sacrifice of a goat, so the brahman picked a goat from his herd and instructed his pupils to take the goat to the river, wash it, feed it grain, groom it, put flowers around its neck, and bring it back for the sacrifice. As all of these preparations were being carried out at the river the goat contemplated its former lives, and suddenly it laughed out loud. Then, just as suddenly, it began to cry loudly. The perplexed pupils asked the goat why it first laughed and then cried without apparent reason. The goat promised to explain if the pupils would restate the question in the presence of their brahman teacher.

When this was done, the goat explained that long, long ago it had also been a learned brahman who had undertaken to honor his ancestors with the ritual sacrifice of a goat: "To exhaust the bad karma from that one violent deed I have been destined to be born five hundred times as a goat and to have my head cut off each time. I laughed with joy when I realized that this was the last of my five hundred births, so after today I will be freed from this curse and can again be reborn in a happy state. Then I thought about how you, brahman, would suffer a similar fate for the violence you are about to do me, and I wept out of compassion for you." The brahman was overcome by the speech and said, "Do not be afraid, because I have decided not to kill you." "Whether you kill me or not, I am destined to die today and obtain release," the goat explained.

The brahman insisted upon protecting the goat, so he ordered his pupils to follow it around to keep it from being harmed. But the brahman's protection was no match for the powers of karmic destiny, and the goat's head was cut off by a piece of flying rock propelled by a bolt of lightning.

This unusual event attracted a large crowd; and the Future Buddha, who had been born as a spirit of a tree in that area, decided to instruct the crowd on the virtue of non-violence. He warned them in a poetic verse about the strict punishment which comes from killing. The people were converted to the dharma of non-violence that day. For the rest of their lives they did good deeds rather than evil ones, and in the end they were rewarded in heaven.

The story of the goat reveals a crucial difference between early Buddhism and the Hinduism of old India. Like the Hebrew, Greek, Chinese, and so many other ancient religions, the Hindus practiced animal sacrifices as an important part of their spirituality. But the Buddhists condemned animal sacrifices and backed this teaching with the threat of a miserable rebirth in hell or on earth as an animal or ghost. Furthermore, the Buddhists shunned the warrior ideals evident in the Hindu story of Abhimanyu and told stories such as the following about kings who ruled well even without executing criminals or waging wars. Theirs was not the courage of the warrior but the courage to remain non-violent, even unto death.

King Goodness Refuses To Fight

Once when Brahmadatta was king of Banaras the Future Buddha came to birth in the womb of the chief wife of the king, and at his naming ritual he was called Prince Goodness. Later he became a king and ruled with extraordinary righteousness and charity. King Goodness established places for feeding the poor at the four city gates, the palace, and the market. He kept all the moral rules and regularly fasted on holy days. He was patient and cherished all the people and animals in his kingdom as a father cherishes his children.

When a courtier "misbehaved" in the king's harem and the matter became public, King Goodness banished the man, who in turn found employment in the court of the king of Kosala. The exiled man advised the king of Kosala to capture King Goodness's realm, predicting that the non-violent king would refuse to defend it. The Kosalan king found the idea incredible, but agreed to send a raiding party as a test. The party was captured after some killing and plundering in a border village, and when they were brought before King Goodness, he asked them to promise not to make any more raids and sent them home with gifts! The Kosalan king sent out two more raiding parties with similar results before deciding to march upon Banaras itself.

As the Kosalan army marched toward the capital, King Goodness's generals pleaded for permission to defend the land, but the king refused and ordered the gates to the city opened. The Kosalan king led his army into the city, bound the soldiers and the king, and buried them alive up to their necks in the burial grounds, expecting jackals to eat their heads off in the night. When the jackals came, the king of the jackals approached King Goodness, who lifted his head to expose his neck. But this was a trick. As the jackal charged, the king seized its neck with his teeth and held on until the jackals promised to withdraw.

Having escaped the grave the king was asked to settle a dispute between two ogres over a corpse they both wished to eat.

The king agreed and requested some favors first. The ogres brought him the food, robes, sword, and other things which had been laid out for his usurper in the palace. With the sword he split the corpse in two, awarding each ogre half. Then the grateful ogres magically transported him past the palace guards into the royal bedroom where the Kosalan king was sleeping. King Goodness awakened the usurper by a blow on the stomach with the flat side of his sword. The startled king asked how King Goodness had gotten past his guards, and upon hearing the explanation the usurper repented having taken advantage of such a genuinely good king. He swore an oath of friendship and apologized before his army and the townspeople.

King Goodness explained to his court that he was successful in the end because he persevered in the way of non-violence and virtue, and he encouraged them to do the same. When he died he was rewarded according to his many merits.

~~~~~

King Goodness managed to maintain his sipiritual purity and still meet his many responsibilities. We turn now to stories about others who attempted to maintain personal purity under difficult circumstances.

PURITY
Hindu Stories

Purity in the Hindu context refers to both the physical and moral condition of a person. From the earliest times, rituals of physical cleanliness and spiritual purity were obligatory for the victim and participants of the Vedic sacrifice. Those rituals included fasting, washing, haircutting, and other physical acts of cleansing as well as prayers, meditation, yogic breathing, and other actions designed to cleanse spiritually the person or animal.

Given the Hindu world view in which moral laws (*dharma*) are also conceived as universal, cosmic laws, what people do physically affects their moral condition and vice versa.

In many stories, particularly devout prayer or meditation can cause physical changes in the immediate environment or throughout the cosmos. For example, in the story that follows, the queen's purity is capable of altering the usual effects of fire.

A Test of Fire

When Rama and his allies had defeated the evil King Ravana, Rama sent for his wife Sita who had languished in Ravana's castle as his captive. As Sita was brought on a couch befitting her royal status, the crowd gossiped suspiciously about her stay with King Ravana and the possibility of her infidelity. Hearing the crowds' suspicions, Rama responded angrily.

"A woman's protector is not her archer, a high wall, or a screened-in tower. Rather, her conduct is her best defense. . . . And Sita, my queen, who has long endured the prison of Ravana should now drop her veil and show her face since I now am by her side to protect her. Let her come down from her vehicle and walk proudly among the people."

With Rama's words, Sita's joy turned to sadness, for it was clear that her husband had been offended by the rumors of infidelity and now insisted that she walk to him as a commoner would. Dutifully, Sita lowered her veil and her head as she approached her lord. Rama, angrily continued:

"Woman, I have done my duty toward you; the prize of this war has been won. . . . It was not for love that I rescued you from across the sea, nor was it for you that my army spilled its blood on foreign soil. I fought to regain my honor which Ravana soiled with your capture, and my love for you has fled because of the stain on your character caused by your relationship with Ravana. Go wherever you choose. The world is open to you and

I set you free! How could I take you home again with me? My friends and relatives would scorn my rule as tainted now that you have been subjected to the lustful gazes and amorous advances of Ravana."

Sita replied in a trembling voice: "How can you who call yourself a ruling prince dismiss a wife of equal status with such mean words? By my virtuous life I swear that I am not what you make me out to be! Because some women are faithless, would you find fault in all? . . . To be sure, I lay in the arms of the mighty Ravana—by his force—and I dreaded those lustful advances. Yet not once did my heart or body become his. I was always faithful unto you.

"Why did you not just leave me with Ravana? . . . I will not bear the shame of your rejection in lonely wanderings. Prepare a funeral pyre for me. I will not live to bear the shame of your rebuff."

A pyre of wood was prepared and lit. Sita ritually walked around her husband and, before entering the fire, made this plea:

"Fire, you universal witness, if I have never left the path of virtue nor been unfaithful to my husband Rama, then protect my body upon the pyre. Free me from Rama's charge of infidelity and aid my virtuous cause."

To the sound of loud wailing from those who loved her, Sita entered the fire. Rama's eyes overflowed with tears for the wife he still loved deeply. He had felt such joy at the return of his beloved wife, but his sense of honor and righteousness kept him from receiving her into his arms. Now his joy at her return had turned to grief as he watched the flames encircle her. But the fire responded to her declaration of virtue, and the lovely Sita emerged unharmed from the flames. Rama joyfully received her, for her virtue was proven, and they returned to the palace to reign in peace.*

---

* In other versions this famous story ends less happily with Sita being "swallowed up" by the earth after a second rejection by Rama.

The Hindu notion of purity extends not only to the realms of physical and spiritual proprieties but also to the realm of social relationships. Since a person's social position is determined by birth, the various classes are not just social conveniences, according to Hindu traditions, but are part of the natural ordering of the cosmos. Therefore, religious purity laws dictate with whom one may eat and whom one may marry, as the following traditional Hindu folktale illustrates.

The Suitable Husband

After King Vikram had again retrieved the goblin from the branches of the graveyard's tree, the goblin posed yet another predicament in story form:

"There was once a city called Shringaravati which was ruled by King Virabahu and his wife Padmavati. The royal couple had two children, a son and a daughter. The daughter, Anangavati, one day said to her father, 'Father, you must give me in marriage to a man endowed with courage, generosity, and goodness,' and the king agreed. In a matter of time, four young princes appeared before King Virabahu to ask for his daughter's hand in marriage. Each of them was brave and handsome. One, head of the servant class (*shudra*), said, 'Your majesty, I am well known for my good qualities and courage.' The second prince said, 'I am a trader (*vaishya*) and am wealthy because of my knowledge of my Vedic duties and my skill in the ways of animals.' The third suitor responded, 'I am the heroic son of a warrior (*kshatriya*) who is knowledgeable in matters of warfare and renowned for my courage.' The fourth young prince rejoined, 'I am a priest (*brahman*), and I am familiar with all the sacred lore and schools of wisdom, not to mention my personal qualities of merit.' Realizing that all four young men were suitable, King Virabahu was perplexed."

The goblin then posed the same question to King Vikram that

107

he had been asking himself: "To whom is Anangavati to be given in marriage?"

King Vikram responded: "Listen goblin, the vaishya and shudra are to be rejected in any marriage of high standing. The brahman is a suitable person, but a warrior and a warrior alone should marry a woman of the warrior class."

~~~~~

As this story implies, the traditional Hindu purity laws act as a sanction against marriages between social groups. To marry someone outside one's own birth group would pollute the family line and alter the very design of the cosmos.

Buddhist Stories

Inner purity is essential to spiritual development according to Buddhist teaching. No significant progress toward perfection and release from the wheel of rebirths is possible without the first step of spiritual development, the practice of basic moral principles. With this in mind, Buddhists at worship reaffirm the five basic vows kept by all lay people and monks (see the "five duties" listed previously). Those who are ordained as monks or nuns are bound by over two hundred other rules of conduct, and at special meetings on holy days they confess any misconduct they may have committed.

For the lay person, sexual relations within marriage are not in any way frowned upon, but for the monk the vow of sexual abstinence implies strict celibacy, in accordance with the very ancient Indian principle that ascetics, monks, and other such holy men should avoid completely all contact with women. A Buddhist monk should not even touch a woman unless it is absolutely necessary (for example, to save her from drowning). In the following story a young ascetic breaks his state of celibacy as a result of an elaborate plan devised by the god Sakka.

How a Youth Lost His Virtue

Once when Brahmadatta was king of Banaras the Future Buddha was born into a wealthy brahman family of the north. When he matured, he departed from the worldly life and became a forest ascetic. Once when he was bathing in a pond near his hut some of his semen mingled with water which was subsequently drunk by a doe. The doe fell in love with the hermit and miraculously conceived via the semen.

When the doe gave birth to a human boy, the sage named him Supreme Sage and raised him in the forest. The boy grew quite adept at meditation and was extraordinarily virtuous and pure. The power of the youth's virtue had become so great by the time he was in his teens that the throne of the god Sakka once more became hot. As usual, Sakka surveyed the world to determine whose virtue was causing this threat to his rule. Seeing that Supreme Sage was the cause, Sakka devised a plan to bring about his fall from purity.

The first part of the god's plan was to withhold rain from the Ganges area for three growing seasons. The people became so desperate that they appealed to their king to bring rain. The king tried prayer and fasting, but with no results. Then the god appeared to the king at night and falsely blamed the drought on Supreme Sage. The king naturally asked how to release the sage's hold on the rains, and Sakka suggested that the king send his daughter into the forest to seduce the young man. The king reluctantly agreed in order to save his kingdom.

The next day he had a father-to-daughter talk with her about things unmentionable under normal circumstances. She agreed to carry out the plan and soon left with an escort for the Himalayan forest.

Camping near the hermitage, the king's men waited until the elder sage had left for the day and then sent the princess toward the hut disguised as a young male ascetic playing with a ball. In his innocence Supreme Sage had never before seen a ball or a woman, and he asked, "What is the name of the tree where you got that fruit which bounces back to you and does not break?" She lied to him, saying that where her hermitage was located there were many wonderful kinds of fruit trees. Supreme Sage was pleased to have a friend in the forest and invited the soft-skinned ascetic into his hut.

Once inside she told him a strange story, saying that once when she was gathering roots and fruits in the forest she crossed paths with a dreadful bear. "It attacked me and clawed off my organ, leaving this deep wound which troubles me with an awful itch. No matter what I do, I can get no relief from the itching. It makes my ascetic task difficult to obtain, Sir."

"Is there anything that I could do for you?" the kind sage replied. She then showed him the "wound" which the bear had made at the top of her thighs, and he said, "This deep wound is red, fragrant, and very large. I will make some yellow-salve yoga in order that you may become well again."

"Oh no," she replied, "no chant-yoga, yellow-salve yoga, nor herbal remedy can bring me pleasure. The cause of the itch can only be removed by something soft. Only in that way can I be well again."

Believing her, the naïve sage was led into sexual intercourse, and as a result his state of moral purity was destroyed and his meditational consciousness was broken. The two had sexual relations for hours, and then the sage bathed in the pond and put on his bark robe once more. The girl made an excuse for leaving and gave him false directions for coming to her own hut another day.

At dusk the young sage's father returned and asked why his son had not cut wood, brought water, and built a fire as usual. The son enthusiastically described the stranger who had spent the day with him. He mentioned the stranger's beautiful black hair, his smooth, beardless cheeks, pretty necklace, round golden breasts, jewelry, soft limbs, and of course the magic bouncing fruit. Then he told his father of the games they played and the

110

bath in the pond. Finally he told how eager he was to journey to the place where this stranger lived.

The wise father realized what had happened and gently instructed the boy never to associate with such a person again, for to do so sweeps away an ascetic's purity as flood waters wash ripe grain from the stalk. The father's explanation led the young sage to conclude that he had encountered an evil female spirit, and he returned to his meditation with renewed vigor.

In the previous story we are able to see the radical tension which exists in the minds of ascetics between celibate purity and sexual indulgence. The ascetics' way to purity, strict celibacy, does not apply to laymen, who have other spiritual means available. The most common Buddhist practice is that of doing meritorious works, or as it is usually translated in English, "making merit." For Buddhists, works of merit may take external forms such as participating in rituals or festivals, giving food to monks, or keeping the moral rules, but the essence of merit is said to be always a matter of the mind, of mental purification. Keep this in mind as you read the following story about a conflict between the Buddha and a brahman who, like millions of Hindus, puts his faith in the purificatory powers of India's sacred rivers.

The Brahman and the Sacred River

Once when the Buddha was instructing a gathering of people in a shady park near a city, a pious brahman approached the Buddha and sat down at his side. The brahman was in the habit of taking regular ritual baths for spiritual purification in the nearby river, which he held to be sacred. Since he suspected that the Buddha's teaching and practice ignored this ancient custom, he asked pointedly, "Do you, honorable Gautama, go down to the Bahuka River to bathe?"

"Why the Bahuka River, brahman? What will that river do for you?" the Buddha asked.

The startled brahman replied, "Gautama, people esteem the Bahuka as a means of liberation—a means of merit, a way to wash away the stain of bad works [*karma*]."

Then Buddha instructed the brahman, saying that the Bahuka River and even more famous rivers can do nothing to purify the evil doer. What can any river do to appease one's guilt? Those who are already pure, he continued, do not need special places to wash or special days. For them every place and day are holy. "Bathe in doing good works, brahman, and you will bring security to all creatures, and not just yourself. Do not lie, kill, or steal, and if you are generous to others, you will be pure. What else can a river do besides providing water, like a well?"

"This is excellent, clear, enlightening teaching," responded the brahman, who then asked to be formally received into the Order of Buddha's followers. The Buddha accepted him and administered the ordination, in which the brahman repeated three times the formula, "I go to the Buddha for my refuge, I go to the Dharma for my refuge, I go to the Order for my refuge." After a few months of meditation and advancement in spiritual insight, the brahman realized the goal of the spiritual path.

The above story is typical of many in the Buddhist scriptures. They tell of Hindus, often high-status, well-educated ones, who respond to the Buddha's emphasis upon inner purification, as opposed to external rituals or prayers of petition to gods. Later, the way of the Buddha was referred to as the "path to purification" by one of Buddhism's most famous commentators, Buddhaghosa.

GENEROSITY
Hindu Stories

The lay Hindu practices generosity primarily by giving gifts to various religious leaders. A teacher's gift (*guru daksina*) is traditionally given by the student or householder to the spiritual teacher (*guru*) for his services. Such a gift is both a payment for services and a way to honor the preceptor. In a different context, brahman ascetics who have renounced the world and who come to a home for food are to be given alms by householders. Such alms provide sustenance for the brahman wanderer, and the generous act of giving acquires merit for the donor. This religious institution of giving to holy men, for mutual benefit, is clear in the following stories.

The Gift of Cows

There once lived a great king named Shivi. He was a strong protector of his people and claimed victory over all of his foes. He performed many sacrifices during which he made generous gifts to all the brahmans present. During his long reign, King Shivi acquired great wealth and the respect of his fellow kings and warriors. During his many horse sacrifices, King Shivi gave away thousands of golden ornaments, elephants, horses, sheep, and baskets of grain. But of all his gifts, none were more blessed or numerous than his gifts of cows. As a symbol of the benefits of the earth herself, the cow was considered the best gift of all. And the cows King Shivi gave away were as numerous as drops of rain, or the stars in the heavens, or the sands of the Ganges River. Even the creator of the earth had not seen any king of the past, or of the future, who could match the liberality of Shivi.

In the sacrifices of King Shivi, all the instruments and furniture of the ritual were made of gold and were given to the priests

113

afterwards. Every imaginable kind of food and drink was available in abundance. The brahmans came from all the territories around to share in the king's kindnesses, and the only phrases heard on those occasions were "give away!" and "take!" Inside the holy confines, where lakes of milk and curds were to be found, the words rang out, "Bathe, drink, and eat as much as you want."

Pleased with King Shivi's righteous deeds, the lord of all the earth granted Shivi a boon: "Just as you have given away your wealth, let your wealth increase. To the extent that you have been generous, let your devotion, fame, and religious acts be inexhaustible." And when King Shivi died, he ascended into heaven to enjoy further rewards as the result of his benevolence.

~~~

The story of King Shivi seems to make clear the process by which a layperson can achieve heaven. "Give to all priests who call at your door and heaven will be your reward," is its logic. The story of King Nirga which follows, however, shows the difficulties that may arise if one improperly shares with wandering priests, even if unknowingly.

A Mistaken Gift

Once while playing near a dry well, some boys found a beautiful lizard. As they brought the lizard near Krishna, it immediately assumed its true form as a celestial king named Nirga. When asked why he had been so unfortunate as to be born a lizard, King Nirga replied that his generosity to a brahman had gotten him into his predicament.

King Nirga explained that in his previous birth he had been a righteous king accustomed to supporting all the wandering sages and priests who came to his door. His typical gift was cattle. But trouble began one day when the cow of a renowned brahman strayed into the king's cattle pen. Later when a wandering priest came begging, the king gave him all the cattle in his pen. When the priest whose cow had been wrongly given away asked the king for his cow, the king could not return it, and the angry priest called him a thief. The king asked the priest to whom he had given his cows if he could have back the one cow that he had had no right to give, and the priest called the king a false giver!

When King Nirga died a few days later, he was allowed to choose whether to ascend immediately to heaven or first to work off the only bad deed of his life, that is, the gift of a cow which had not been his to give.

The king had chosen to suffer first for his one evil deed, and consequently had been reborn as a lizard. Upon his release by Krishna's presence, King Nirga ascended to heaven where he lived a long time.

∼∼∼

While King Nirga's generosity finally merited him a long life in heaven, the story of his plight at the hand of an offended brahman exposes the priestly bias of the story teller. As we have already seen, brahmans consider themselves to be the highest social class, and the stories incorporate their claims to power and prestige. Story after story in India reveals brahmans' feelings of superiority and reflects their high achievements or their harmful pride. In King Nirga's case, even a generous act based on good intentions had harmful consequences due to two brahmans' pride.

Buddhist Stories

Gifts given to holy men were the main avenue of generosity for Buddhist as well as Hindu laymen, but as Buddhism developed the ordained monk replaced the wandering brahman as the proper recipient of the householder's gifts. The pattern that developed in old India and spread with Buddhism to other countries was that the monks rise at dawn and walk silently through the

115

village in quest of alms. Housewives come to the street and put rice and other food into the monk's almsbowl. Then the monk returns to the monastery to eat his only full meal of the day. In this way the monks are freed of the necessity of earning a livelihood and the laity gains merit. On birthdays, high holy days, and other special occasions larger gifts such as cloth for robes, equipment for the monastery, or even new buildings are given.

The following stories present models of generosity as practiced by a prince, a merchant, and a servant girl. The first is from the longest and most popular of all the *Jatakas*, the stories of the Buddha's former lives. It has been illustrated on temple walls in every Buddhist country and is retold at certain festivals.

The King Who Gave Away His Kingdom

Once the Future Buddha was born into a royal family of great virtue as a prince named Vessantara. At his birth he announced to his mother that he wished to make some gifts, and she provided him with pieces of gold which he in turn gave away. On that same day a white [albino] elephant was born in the royal stable, and since white elephants are very rare and very lucky, it was treated royally.

Even as a little boy the prince gave away everything that his father bestowed upon him. Then when he was eight he vowed to give away anything that was asked for, even his eye or his heart. His generosity continued as he matured.

A nearby kingdom was troubled by drought and in desperation its king sent a delegation of brahmans to beg for Vessantara's lucky white elephant. He cheerfully gave the beast to them, even though it had brought good fortune to his whole kingdom. The citizens were very angry with the prince for giving away the lucky elephant, and they complained bitterly to the king. At last the king submitted to their demand that the prince be banished from the kingdom. But before leaving Vessantara gave the "gift of seven hundreds" [he gave seven hundred maidens, cows, horses, etc., to many eager recipients].

The prince's wife insisted upon going into the forest with him, although the delicate princess was ill-prepared for the rough forest life. So the prince, the princess, and their children rode out of the city in a royal chariot pulled by well-bred horses.

Some brahmans who arrived too late for the prince's massive giveaway consoled themselves by begging the horses and chariot—his last possessions. The family traveled on foot under the protection of the gods and eventually reached the Himalaya region where hermits dwell. Then they began to live as ascetics in a hermitage provided by the god Sakka. The princess rose early each morning and brought water and toothsticks before going in search of roots and fruits. The prince remained at the hermitage in meditation through the day. At night the princess slept apart from the prince, at his request, according to the tradition that ascetics be celibate.

Trouble arose when a brahman sought out the hermit family and begged to have the children as slaves for his wife. As the generous Vessantara gave him the children, the earth itself quaked from the power of his spirituality, and he wished that by this most difficult gift he might at last win the state of perfect mind. The children were bound and beaten by the cruel brahman, even before they were out of their father's sight. The heartbroken Vessantara went into his hut and wept bitterly as the cries of his children faded into the distance. Meanwhile the gods detained the children's mother in the forest until nightfall. When she returned to the hut and asked where her children were, Vessantara could not bring himself to answer. Frantically, the mother searched the moonlit forest, but the brahman had taken them far away by then. She searched through the night and collapsed from exhaustion at dawn. Vessantara was afraid she might be dead and, readily breaking his vow, he caressed her and splashed water on her face to revive her. When she regained consciousness, he explained that the children had been given to a poor

117

brahman, and she was relieved to at least hear that they were not dead. "Somehow they will be returned to us," he promised, "but for now I had to give them away. I cannot refuse a brahman's request."

Even more trouble came the very next day. Another old brahman came and asked Vessantara for his wife. At first Vessantara despaired at the thought of separation from his wife, but he summoned his courage and performed a ritual in which he poured water over his right hand as a seal of the gift of his wife to the brahman. The princess dutifully left her husband and prepared to leave with the brahman when an unexpected turn of fortune took place.

The old brahman revealed that he was the god Sakka disguised for the purpose of testing Vessantara's generosity, and he immediately returned the woman to Vessantara and promised him eight boons as a reward for his generosity. Vessantara wished for: reconciliation with his father and a return to his kingdom as the king, the power to rule without the need of capital punishment, the power to help his subjects, the moral strength to avoid adultery, long life for his son, food for his subjects, the means to support his continued generosity, and liberation from rebirth on earth.

Meanwhile, the gods confused the brahman who had been given the children into traveling toward the palace where their grandfather the king gladly ransomed them from slavery. The king then set out to find his son and turn the kingdom over to him. When the children were united with their virtuous mother the earth shook again. The united royal family journeyed back to the palace, where the new king reigned in peace and prosperity. Sakka caused gold and jewels to be unearthed to replenish the royal treasury which Vessantara's generosity frequently emptied.

Generosity is a value to be practiced not just by kings and forest sages but by others as well, as the following story of a generous businessman illustrates. It reminds us of the biblical character, Job, another righteous man who was tested.

The Buddhist Job

Once when Brahmadatta was king of Banaras the Future Buddha lived as an extremely wealthy merchant named Visayha. He was a virtuous man who kept the five basic rules of morality and was extremely generous. He endowed an alms-hall [for distributing free food] at each of the four city gates, in the middle of the city, and at his residence, and thousands of hungry people were fed each day. He personally helped distribute the food and ate exactly the same food that he gave to the poor.

The power of the merit the rich merchant was accumulating was so great that the yellow, marble throne of the god Sakka began to heat up, and once again the god turned his attention to the earth to see who the pretender to his own throne might be. Seeing that Visayha was the meritorious one, Sakka took radical measures. With his divine capabilities he caused Visayha's stored food to perish and all his wealth to disappear. The situation was so grave that when a beggar came to their door, Visayha and his wife could find nothing whatsoever to give in charity.

In desperation Visayha turned to manual labor. He found an old scythe and worked until he had cut two bundles of hay, which he sold for two pennies intending to give one as alms and to buy food for himself and his wife with the other. But many beggars came along, so Visayha gave away both coins and went without any food that day. And so it went until Visayha collapsed from hunger. At that point Sakka appeared and tempted the weakened man to cease his practice of extreme charity.

"Who are you, anyway?" Visayha asked the tempter. "I am Sakka," came the reply, at which Visayha spoke his mind.

"Sakka! Why, you yourself got your office by means of charity, observing the fast days and keeping the moral rules. How can you of all people thwart someone else's good deeds? You are quite wrong to do this."

Without denying the charge against him, Sakka asked Visayha what goal lay behind all his almsgiving. "I am not interested in being a god such as Sakka or Brahma," Visayha informed the relieved Sakka, "rather, I am after perfect wisdom." When he had heard this good news, Sakka touched the weak merchant and his health miraculously returned, along with endless wealth.

Visayha and his wife resumed their charities and Sakka returned to his heavenly throne.

To make merit is an important goal for Buddhists, and the generous giving of food and other requisites to monks remains a major means of attaining that goal. Buddhist laymen and laywomen are encouraged to overcome all *evil* desires, but the desire to make merit and enjoy the corresponding heavenly reward is quite acceptable, according to stories such as the following.

A Mansion in Heaven

During the days when Lord Buddha was a traveling teacher, he happened to be in the vicinity of Thuna, a village of brahmans who were staunch supporters of traditional religion and opponents of Buddha's teachings. When the villagers heard that he was coming, they agreed to withhold all hospitality from him in order to discourage him from remaining in their area. They were too pious to cause him harm, but they did remove the boats from the village dock, blocked the bridges, polluted the wells with rubbish, and closed down the area rest houses.

Lord Buddha intuited their strange behavior and took compassion on them; he decided to go teach among them despite their stubborn resistance. He and his disciples crossed the river by levitation and sat down under a tree in the village. The village women, determined to withhold hospitality, did not offer him water. A non-brahman servant girl broke the agreement, however, for she was generous and she also saw what an opportunity this was to obtain a better life for herself in the future. She knew that an enlightened person was a great merit-field, for gifts to a holy man produce great fruit, like seed sown in an extremely fertile field.

Though the girl knew that she would be punished by her master, she respectfully approached the Buddha, saluted him reverently, and gave him water for drinking and washing. To her amazement the water jar remained full, so she proceeded to give water to all the disciples as well and then returned home with a water jar still filled to the brim, meditating on the joyous occasion. When her master heard of her deed, he beat her so mercilessly that she died.

The next day the Buddha and his disciples were again thirsty, so he miraculously caused water to gush up from the wells, at once cleansing them and flooding the village. The awestruck villagers converted to the Buddha's teaching. At the celebration the following day, another miracle occurred. A beautiful angel approached through the sky on a magic boat. The people were spellbound by her radiance and her large retinue of servants. They eagerly asked her what deed had merited such a heavenly reward.

The angel identified herself as the former servant girl and described her mansion in the heavens as a large property having many buildings with high-peaked roofs, lotus ponds, a pleasant river with pure water and white, sandy beaches, and a magic tree able to grant all her wishes. All this splendor and her own beauty was her reward for giving water to thirsty holy men, she explained, and added that anyone who, with the right attitude, did likewise could expect a similar reward.

The Buddha then gave instructions concerning truth, and the

angel achieved the first level of spiritual attainment, known as "entering the stream to nirvana" before returning to her mansion in heaven.

⟍⟋

These Buddhist stories idealize giving gifts to holy men and to the poor. In general, Buddhists consider the act of giving provisions for the Order (*Sangha*) of monks the more meritorious because of the great merit of the recipients, but gifts to the poor are also thought to be an important expression of compassion.

SELF-SACRIFICE
Hindu Stories

Servanthood is one context for self-sacrifice in India. However, it is not only the servant class whose relationship to superior classes requires self-negating behavior out of respect for a master; all citizens are servants of the king. Here servanthood is not a status determined by birth, but is a politically and socially derived role which may change throughout a person's life. (One difference is that people born servants are governed by laws (*dharma*) which ensure that the servant will always bow in service before all other superior classes, while religious or political servitude is relative with respect to the status of the other citizens of the kingdom.) For example, a warrior serves the king as a serf yet demands respect and service from merchants, whom he views as lower residents of the king's realm. In the story which follows, a warrior's service is interpreted to include even the sacrifice of his life on behalf of his kingly master—a demanding model indeed.

Death's Substitute

As King Vikram once again hoisted the goblin on his shoulder, his passenger told this riddle:

"There once was a king named Shudraka who had the attributes of a world ruler. As he sat surrounded by his ministers one day, a warrior from a foreign country came to Shudraka's gate with his wife and children and told the gatekeeper he had heard of King Shudraka's renown and had come seeking employment. The warrior was presented to the king saying, 'My name is Viravara ["Best of heroes"] and I am a warrior. I have come here to ask that I may serve you.' The king asked, 'What salary do you require?' The stranger replied, 'Your majesty should give me fifteen hundred pieces of gold a day.' The startled king retorted, 'I know of many good men with excellent qualities, but none of them commands so high a salary.'

"One of the king's ministers advised Shudraka, 'Don't shrink from testing Viravara's merit. Pay him what he asks at least for a few days. Your money will not be wasted.' So the king gave Viravara the position of a palace guard at the salary he had demanded. Viravara's response was to give half of his pay each day to the brahmans, a quarter to some orphans, and a quarter he used to support himself and his family. The king was pleased by the warrior's generosity and kept him in his service.

"One night the king heard a mournful wail outside the castle gate to the south and called out, 'Is the gatekeeper there?' Viravara responded, 'O Lord, I am here.' The king said, 'Viravara, who is the woman who is crying? Find out and report to me.' Viravara left to do the king's bidding. The king also went out secretly to observe the honesty of his highly paid palace guard.

"When Viravara found the woman who was crying he asked, 'Respected mother, why are you alone and weeping?' The woman responded, 'Son, I am King Shudraka's destiny personified. That great-souled ruler will die at dawn. So I am crying for myself, for then I will have no form in which to reside.' The warrior replied, 'Good woman, tell me what can be done to prevent the king from dying and to provide long life for you; I will do as you say.' The woman, who was really the goddess of good fortune in disguise, said, 'To prevent the king's death will require uncommon sacrifice.' Viravara answered, 'I will do the impossible if it will save the king.' The goddess continued, 'Bring a son endowed with auspicious marks whose mother and sister are willing to hold his feet and whose father is willing to sacrifice his son to the goddess Devi. After the boy is dragged by the hair, and his head is cut off, the king's life will be spared.' Saying this, the woman disappeared. The king, who had heard the whole discussion, followed Viravara as he left.

"When Viravara returned and told his family what he had learned his wife responded, 'If we do not assist in the performance of this difficult task, how will we be liberated in our next birth?' Viravara's son said, 'I am fortunate since my death will provide a whole kingdom with good leadership for years to come.' The daughter too consented. And all the while the king stood outside Viravara's door listening.

"The family went to Devi's temple, and performed the sacrifice precisely as the strange woman had instructed. Having sacrificed his own son that the king might live, Viravara then cut off his own head out of grief for his son and in the hope that an additional sacrifice would doubly ensure the king's safety. The wife and daughter followed Viravara by sacrificing themselves too. Having seen all that had taken place, King Shudraka started to cut off his own head out of remorse for his loyal warrior and his family. Immediately, a voice came out of heaven and said, 'Oh King, don't give yourself as an offering, the goddess is pleased with you.' The king responded, 'Oh Goddess, if that be so, then let Viravara and his family live again.'

"Restored to life, Viravara took his family home and then went to see the king. The king came out to greet him saying, 'Viravara, what took you so long? Who was that woman crying?'

124

Viravara replied, 'Dear lord, an unhappy woman was weeping and I sent her away.' The king sent Viravara home. The next day the king told all his ministers of the heroism of Viravara and his family, and all of them were astonished. As a reward for Viravara's loyalty, King Shudraka gave the prized warrior many horses, elephants, servants, and treasures and made him king of a realm of his own."

The goblin then challenged King Vikram, "Who is the greater hero, King Shudraka or his warrior Viravara?" Vikram replied, "Listen goblin. It is the rule for servants that they lay down their life for their master. King Shudraka is the greater hero since by his willingness to sacrifice himself he was able to bring life to Viravara and his family and to bestow a whole kingdom as a reward."

A second Indian context in which self-sacrifice is a required behavior is that of *bhakti* or "devotional" Hinduism. Often called the "popular" religion of India, the theistic traditions of devotional Hinduism promise a heavenly salvation to all who surrender their lives to an all-powerful deity (usually a form of Vishnu or Shiva). The *Bhagavad Gita* (9.27) expresses succinctly the devotional norm of self-giving, "Whatever you do, whatever you eat, whatever you offer in sacrifice or give, whatever self-controlling behavior you perform, do that as an offering to me (Vishnu)." This complete devotion is required of all devotees, regardless of social class. In the devotional context, all persons—king, merchant, and serf—are considered equal before the throne of the highest god. In the story that follows, a poor brahman makes an extraordinary sacrificial gift to his boyhood friend Krishna, who is actually the full incarnation of the god Vishnu.

A Handful of Rice

Shridama had been a boyhood playmate of Krishna, and now Krishna was the ruler of Dvaraka while Shridama was a poor household priest. Shridama had mastered the Vedic lore and had rejected sensual, worldly delights in order to perfect his simple religious life. His wife, too, shared her husband's poor life as they both ate only what others had to spare and were dressed in discarded rags. One day, Shridama's wife came to her husband saying, "I am weak from hunger and my body trembles from lack of care. You were a boyhood friend of the noble and wealthy lord Krishna. Please go to your childhood friend and tell him of our situation, and he will surely give some of his wealth to an old friend." Again and again, Shridama's wife urged him to seek help from Krishna until Shridama finally made up his mind to it.

Shridama knew that he should take Krishna a gift, but there was nothing of value to be found in his house. He asked his wife, "Do you have anything worthy of being given to Krishna?" His wife had begged four handfuls of flat rice which she bound in a cloth and gave to Shridama. "Take this flat rice to Krishna," she said. "It is all the food we have." So Sridama set off for Krishna's palace with his small gift in hand.

As Shridama entered the city of Dvaraka, he passed by soldiers' huts and came to the gate of Krishna's palace. Meanwhile, Krishna had seen Shridama coming in the distance and ran out to greet his old friend. Krishna embraced Shridama as tears of joy trickled down both their faces. Krishna immediately ordered water to be brought and then washed the feet of Shridama himself—a customary way of honoring a priest. Krishna then smeared sandalwood paste over Shridama's body as he would have done to any royal guest. Then Krishna offered a sumptuous meal to his long lost friend whose body showed signs of a meager diet and whose clothes indicated his poor condition.

After the meal, some time was spent in good-natured remembering of boyhood days together. Then Krishna said, "Good

126

brahman, what gift have you brought for me from your house? Any gift, no matter how small, is appreciated by me when I know that it is given in love. When presents are given to me by those who hold no reverence for me, I am unsatisfied, no matter how grand the gift. So don't be ashamed of what you could afford to bring." [Krishna had perceived that Shridama had come out of love for his friend and not for the purposes his wife had encouraged. Consequently, Krishna had decided to grant prosperity to his friend even though Shridama clearly was not going to ask for it.]

Shridama gingerly pulled out his gift of flat rice bound in a piece of tattered cloth and, without speaking, gave it to Krishna. Krishna responded, "Indeed, my friend, you have brought a truly worthy gift to me and I am grateful. This flat rice is very much to my liking." Saying this, Krishna ate a handful of the flat rice.

That night Shridama spent in the palace of Krishna eating and drinking food his stomach had not known for some time. At dawn, Shridama set off for his own home with the good wishes of Krishna. As he walked along, Shridama reflected on the pleasant visit he had enjoyed with his friend. He had not gotten any gold or silver and he had not even been able to ask for help for his wife and himself. His wife! What would she say now that Shridama had given away their last bit of food and had nothing to show in exchange.

As Shridama came into the vicinity of his own house, he was startled from his musings by the sight of a palace sitting on the spot where his broken-down house had been. Chariots were parked outside the mansion, and soldiers and servants milled about doing the various tasks one would expect at the home of royalty. As Shridama stood perplexed, his wife greeted him joyfully. She considered her husband's journey responsible for their good fortune and fell down at his feet. Still struck with amazement, Shridama embraced his wife as they entered the house together.

When Shridama entered the house he saw seats made of gold, fine linens on the beds, and opulent fixtures wherever he looked.

He thought to himself, "Where can this wealth have come from except that my friend Krishna saw my poverty and gave me of his goods without my even asking. My lord and friend gives this kind of wealth even to those who do not ask, and promises nothing to those who beg from him. May I always freely give regardless of what I have, because none of these fineries are as excellent as love and service to Lord Krishna."

Thereafter, Shridama and his wife lived in regal splendor, but Shridama was not attached to those luxuries.

Buddhist Stories

Buddhist stories idealize self-sacrifice in much the same way as the Hindu stories. However, the Buddhist stories do not stress the idea that a servant should be willing to lay down his life for his master, but rather that *anyone* should be willing to sacrifice himself out of compassion for another.

The Indians imagine the profile of a jumping "hare in the moon" rather than a man in the moon, and the following fable explains what the hare did to deserve the honor.

The Hare in the Moon

Once when Brahmadatta was king of Banaras the Future Buddha was conceived in the womb of a hare in the forest. The baby hare to which she gave birth grew to be very wise and virtuous, and he gave moral instruction to an otter, a jackal, and a monkey, who were his friends. On the eve of one full moon, he told them that the next day was a holy day which they should observe by fasting, and if the opportunity arose, by giving food to a brahman. The other three animals happened across food appropriate to a human, but the hare had no way to obtain human food. With this in mind, he vowed that if a brahman should ask him

128

for food, he would sacrifice himself to the brahman. As he made this vow, the throne of Sakka heated up once more, and Sakka came to earth to test the sincerity of the hare.

Sakka, disguised as a brahman, first begged food at the homes of the other three animals, and they responded generously because the hare had taught them the way of virtue. Then Sakka came to the hare and begged food. The hare was pleased with this opportunity and instructed the brahman to build a fire. When a bed of hot coals was prepared the hare shook himself three times to remove any insects which might be in his fur so that they would not die in the fire, then he joyfully leaped into the bed of coals. But by the power of his virtue the red coals felt like pieces of ice, and he was unharmed. The puzzled hare asked the brahman the meaning of this strange turn of events, and the god replied that it was only a test of his virtue.

As a reward for the hare's self-sacrifice, Sakka marked the image of a hare upon the moon before returning to his heaven. The hare and his three friends continued to live virtuously in the forest for many years.

We have already told a Hindu story about the good King Shivi's willingness to cut off his own flesh as ransom for the pigeon that sought his protection. Now we offer a Buddhist version of King Shivi's self-sacrificing virtue.

The Eye Transplant

Once the Future Buddha was born as the son of the great King Sivi.* When the prince (also named Sivi) came of age, his father retired and he took the throne. The young King Sivi ruled with virtue and extreme generosity. He ordered that six alms-halls be built, one at each of the four city gates, one in the center of the

* The (Buddhist) Pali equivalent of the Sanskrit "Shivi" is "Sivi."

city, and one at the palace. King Sivi had all kinds of good food and clothing distributed to the poor at these six sites, and the people were very content; but Sivi himself was not. "I give away only external things," he thought, "but never anything of myself." Then he vowed that he would give something of himself that day, if asked. He decided that if he were asked for flesh, he would cut off some of his own. If asked for a heart, he would cut open his chest with a spear and pull out his bleeding heart, as if he were pulling a lotus plant from a pond. If asked for an eye, he would gladly pluck one out. Or if asked to do menial labor, he would put on servants' clothing and do the work.

Meanwhile, in heaven the god Sakka knew what King Sivi was thinking and determined to put him to the test. Sakka, disguised as an old, blind brahman, came to the alms-hall that day and held out his hand before the king, saying "Victory to the king." The king asked him what he wanted, and the blind brahman replied, "I have no good eyes, but you have two. Give me an eye and we will each have one."

The king was pleased with this opportunity to fulfill his vow and immediately sent for the royal surgeon. The surgeon and all the courtiers pleaded with the king to change his mind but he would not, so the surgeon made a powder which he placed upon the king's eye. In spite of intense pain the king still refused to change his mind. Again and again the powder was applied until the eye popped out of the socket and dangled down the king's bloodied cheek. Still the king insisted the surgeon go through with the operation, so the connections were cut and the eye was placed in the king's hands. The king then gave the precious gift to the brahman, who put the eye in place. By Sakka's power the transplanted eye worked! The king was so pleased that he ordered the surgeon to transplant his other eye.

Sakka returned to heaven without revealing his identity, and King Sivi returned to his palace to recuperate from the operation. His eye sockets eventually healed, the pain ceased, and he ruled for a while as a blind king.

We have seen that the power of extreme generosity can work miracles, and now we turn to stories about the power of truthfulness. The power of truth figures in the second half of the King Sivi story, so we will continue it in the next section.

TRUTHFULNESS
Hindu Stories

Truthfulness is not simply a mode of speaking, but a way of living according to Indian philosophical and religious literature. It is not enough that what one says is true (since much may have been left unsaid which could alter any given statement), but the person who speaks must likewise be true. Not surprisingly, the Sanskrit noun for truth (*satya*) is derived from a verbal root (*as*) which connotes being or existence. Therefore, a person who lives righteously and truthfully will obviously speak the truth. Moreover, those who live according to the duties of their rank and birth can call upon that truthfulness as a witness for their assertions, as the virtuous Sita did in the story, "A Test of Fire." Earthly goals are likewise achievable, as revealed in this story of Damayanti's engagement to Nala, whose subsequent addiction to gambling was recounted in "Good King Nala's Downfall."

An Act of Truth

The auspicious lunar day arrived when Damayanti was to hold her husband-choosing ceremony, and King Bhima had summoned all of the mighty lords of the earth to this special event. Hearing the summons, even the gods hastened to Damayanti's court, excited at the thought that they might be chosen to be the husband

132

of the slender-waisted princess. The assembled lords entered a great theater with golden columns and shining arches like lions ascending a great mountain. All these renowned princes, decked out with garlands of fragrant flowers and polished, jeweled earrings took seats around the huge hall. The assembled kings resembled a den filled with potent serpents or a mountain cave overfilled with awesome tigers. Their thick arms were strong as iron bars and rippled with the might of five-hooded cobras. The hair and facial features of the kings gave off a radiance like the stars of the heavens.

When Damayanti entered the hall, the assembled suitors were immobilized by her comely form. When the names of the kings were announced, Damayanti was startled to see five men who looked like Nala! As Damayanti looked closer, she could not distinguish which one was the man she really desired. Filled with anxiety, Damayanti thought to herself, "How shall I discern Nala from the four gods who have adopted his form to trick me into choosing them?" With this thought, Damayanti became filled with grief. No matter how hard she looked, she could not see the divine marks celestials were said to possess.

As a last resort, Damayanti turned to the gods themselves. Bowing before the five Nalas, Damayanti said: "From the first time I heard about Nala's might and goodness, I have desired him as my husband. By the truth of these words, Oh gods, reveal him to me. As I have never swayed in heart and mind from my allegiance to him, by this truth, Oh gods, point out Nala to me. And if Nala was destined to be my husband by the gods' own ordination, by that truth show him to me. Let each of you gods reveal his own true form so that I may recognize the lord Nala."

Hearing Damayanti's mournful lament, and responding to her devotion to truth, the gods assumed their distinguishing characteristics. As Damayanti looked up she saw four gods who were free of sweat and did not blink. They wore unwithered garlands, were not dusty, and hovered several inches off the ground. Beside the celestials stood Nala, with his feet on the ground and his

133

eyes blinking. He was dusty, sweating, his garland had wilted and his form cast a shadow on the ground. Now certain of her choice, Damayanti touched the hem of his garment and placed a fresh wreath of flowers around Nala's neck, and with these gestures, Nala was proclaimed the choice of the fair-haired Damayanti.

~~~~~

We have seen that truthfulness provides vindication and reward. Lying likewise brings undesirable consequences. Even though King Yudhishthira makes a statement of fact in the war episode that follows, his intention is to deceive, and it brings him grief. For as we have seen, in Hindu moral law, it is not enough to speak the truth; one must *be* truthful.

The Power of a Lie

On the fifteenth day of the great battle between the two Bharata clans, the Pandava army was being badly routed by its enemies led by the mighty Drona, who had taught battle skills to many of them. Krishna advised them: "This master archer cannot be defeated in common battle—even by the gods. Unless he lays aside his weapons, he will destroy all your army by himself! When he puts down his weapons, he will be as vulnerable as any mortal; so the problem is how to get him to lay down his arms. I suspect that Drona will stop fighting if he believes his son, Ashvatthaman, has been killed. Let someone, therefore, proclaim the death of his son."

The Pandavas argued among themselves about Krishna's advice. Some said that all was fair in war while others argued that a warrior was obliged to maintain his honor even if it meant death. Finally, one Pandava brother, Bhima, decided upon a plan which accepted Krishna's advice. Taking his war club, Bhima struck and killed a huge elephant which had been known as

Ashvatthaman because of its great strength and courage in battle. Having killed Ashvatthaman the elephant, Bhima went to the front line of battle and shouted across to Drona, "Ashvatthaman has been killed. Lay down your arms as a dutiful father should at the time of his son's death."

Drona's limbs became weak and his heart sank at Bhima's words. However, after considering his son's prowess in battle and the ignoble reputation of Bhima, Drona did not lay down his arms. Drona believed that Bhima was lying and fought even harder. With Drona angered, the Pandava army fell like grain before a farmer's sickle. One after another of the Pandava chieftains was slain by Drona's sword, and those remaining were afraid that they and their whole armies would be destroyed. Together they said, "You are fighting unrighteously, honorable Drona. The hour of your son's death has come. Lay down your weapons. . . . You know the Vedic injunctions regarding a brahman's duties, so lay aside your bow and sword and do your fatherly duty."

Drona was again overcome with feelings of grief, but he was still not convinced that he could believe his enemies' reports. Drona knew, however, that Yudhishthira had been sired by the god of righteousness himself (Dharma) and thought that Yudhishthira would not speak an untruth even if the lordship of the three worlds was at stake. Thus he trusted Yudhishthira's word above all others from the camp of the enemy and called out to him to verify the dreadful report.

Yudhishthira didn't know what to do. Krishna advised again, "If Drona fights enraged even for half a day, our armies will be annihilated. Save us from Drona! Under such circumstances, falsehood is better than truth. Telling a falsehood for the sake of saving lives is not a wrong." Listening to Krishna's advice, Yudhishthira answered Drona, "Ashvatthaman—the elephant—is dead." (Since Yudhishthira had whispered the words "the elephant," all Drona heard was "Ashvatthaman . . . is dead.") Drona laid down his arms and was soon killed.

Immediately upon uttering a lie, Yudhishthira's chariot (which previously rode a hand's width above the earth due to his celestial parentage) sank down to the earth, making his head no higher than that of a common soldier. His lie had debased his very nature.

Buddhist Stories

The Buddhists also idealized truthfulness and told stories about the miracles that can be performed by the power of truth, as we have already seen. We will give one more example of a Buddhist Act of Truth because by doing so we can restore poor King Sivi's sight!

The Eye Restored

The generous King Sivi became dissatisfied with himself, thinking, "What good is a blind king?" so he renounced the throne and retired to the royal park where he lived the spiritual life of an ascetic. His virtue and ascetic practices caused Sakka's throne to heat up once more, and as usual the god came to earth to see if the holy person causing the trouble intended to replace him.

Sakka identified himself this time, and granted Sivi a boon. Sivi said that he had already renounced wealth, health, and power, and chose death as his boon. Sakka wisely asked if Sivi really wished to die or if he felt despair at his blindness. Sakka explained to Sivi that he should think more of the future, and advised him to make a declaration of truth about how he became blind. "By such an Act of Truth you can be healed," Sakka assured him.

Sivi declared, "Whatever was asked of me, I always gave it freely and gladly. If this be true, may one of my eyes be restored." Immediately one eye reappeared in Sivi's head and he regained his sight. Then Sivi made a second declaration, "A brahman begged one eye of me, and I joyfully gave him two. If this be true, may I have both eyes restored."

The new eyes were not natural ones, which a god cannot give, and they were not celestial eyes, for heavenly eyes cannot be placed where there is imperfection. Instead they were the eyes of perfect truth, and they could see through things and over things for great distances in all directions. With his fantastic eyes the king returned to rule over the city. He called all the workers together and instructed them never to eat any food without first sharing, if asked. He taught the people how to live according to dharma. They all followed his advice and, when they died, filled the world of the gods.

Just as a solemn declaration of truth can work a miracle, so a falsely sworn oath can have dire consequences. According to Buddhist thought it is possible for a person to be reborn in one of several states of existence, or destinies. The most unpleasant ones are rebirth in hell or as a miserable ghost, as occurs in our next story. The other destinies are rebirth as an animal, a human, or an angel in heaven. In Buddhism, as in Hinduism, one's destiny after death is said to be determined by karma, the psychic power of one's good or evil deeds. In our story the karma of the evil deed causes rebirth as a ghost, which can only be ended by the karma of a good (meritorious) deed. Since ghosts by nature cannot do good deeds, the merit must be made by a human and then ritually transferred to the ghost. After benefiting from the transfer, the ghost in our story is released from its miserable state and reborn in a happier destiny, due to good deeds done in previous lives. The threat of rebirth as a ghost provided a strong motivation toward truthfulness in the minds of those who heard stories such as the following:

The Woman Who Cursed Herself

Once when the Buddha was teaching near the city of Savatthi he told the people the following story. There was once a man in a nearby village who owned a farm that had been in his family for generations. His relatives were worried that the family would lose the farm because the man's wife was barren and there were no sons to inherit the property. His relatives encouraged him to marry a second wife, and his wife insisted that he follow their advice.

Despite her consent to the plan, the first wife became very jealous when the new wife became pregnant. She bribed a student knowledgeable in medicine to abort the baby. The second wife suspected the reason for her abortion and complained to her mother, who in turn called upon her male relatives to exercise their duty to intervene as protectors of the victimized young bride.

When confronted with the accusation of instigating the abortion, the first wife staunchly denied the charge. The accusers nonetheless demanded that she swear her innocence in an oath, which she did in the following words: "If I am guilty of causing this abortion, may I live to eat the flesh of my own children."

When the first wife died shortly thereafter, her evil deed, her perjury, and the power of her curse combined to cause her to be reborn in the body of a miserable ghost. A group of eight Buddhist monks happened to be passing through the woods where she dwelled and were shocked to see such an ugly, stinking figure standing nude in their path. She told them her sad story, explaining that each morning and evening, she gave birth to five children, whom she then gobbled up in a vain attempt to stave off her overwhelming pangs of hunger and thirst.

Taking pity on her, the monks went for alms at the very household where she had formerly lived. After receiving food from the householder, they suggested that he make a ritual statement to the effect that the merit of his almsgiving be transferred to the benefit of the ghost. When this was done, the ghost was released from her curse and, after appearing to her former husband in a dream, passed on to a more pleasant rebirth.

~~~~~

Pride has always been a barrier to truthfulness, and in the following story we learn how yet another human falls victim to it.

Pride Goeth Before a Fall

Once when Brahmadatta was king of Banaras an attack of malaria killed the king's chaplain and all of his family except a small boy. When the orphaned brahman boy grew older he managed to attend the best brahman school of the day, the one at the city named Takkasila. After completing school he decided to travel about India, since he had no family. In his travels he came upon a remote village of chandalas, a low servant class of people, and there he saw a man selling ripe mangoes out of season. He decided to stay a while in the village to learn the secret of this low-class man (who was really the Future Buddha). He secretly followed the man as he left the village early one morning. The chandala went to a mango grove, stood seven paces from a tree, and recited a magical charm. Then he threw water at the tree, which suddenly blossomed and grew fruit. Within minutes beautiful, ripe mangoes fell from the tree to be gathered by the chandala, who started back to the village to sell them.

The brahman youth hurried to the man's house, greeted his wife, and waited for her husband to return, pretending not to know anything about the mango charm. When the man returned with the mangoes, he intuited that the brahman wanted his charm and said on the sly to his wife, "He wants my charm, but it would not last with him because he is no good." The brahman stayed in the house and did the work of a servant, although it was unheard of that a high-caste brahman should serve a chandala.

After he had spent several years bringing water, washing, cooking, and even acting as midwife, the wife said to her husband, "I feel that you should teach him the charm now. For he has performed the lowest of tasks even though he is a high-born youth." The man agreed and taught the charm to the youth, but with these words of caution. "If you are ever asked who taught you the charm you must admit that you learned it from me, a chandala." "Of course I would give you credit as my teacher," the brahman said confidently.

The brahman eagerly returned to Banaras, now that he had a good means of livelihood. He used the charm to get fruit out of season, and the demand was so great in the big city that he soon was rich. One day the king ate one of the mangoes and asked to see the person who could sell such fruit out of season. The king received the brahman politely, then asked, "Do you get them from some supernatural serpent or bird, or from a god?" "No, I have a charm for getting mango trees to bear out of season," came the reply. The king was pleased and appointed him purveyor to the king, which made the youth not only rich but influential.

One day the king asked to be taken along on a mango expedition. So the king and his entourage watched in amazement as the brahman worked the charm. "Who taught you that charm?" the king inquired. The brahman remembered his teacher's warning, but by now he had repeated the charm so often that he knew he would never forget it. Too proud to admit that he, a brahman, had worked for a village chandala in order to get the charm, he said, "I earned it from a renowned brahman teacher at Takkasila."

The very next day the king went again to the mango grove to see the miracle. This time nothing happened even though the brahman repeated the words and gestures over and over. The brahman was ashamed of himself, for he knew that by his lie he had lost the charm. The king called out, "What is the matter?" and the desperate brahman made the excuse that the stars were not in the right position. "You never mentioned stars before," the

140

king pointed out. "You are right," the fallen brahman admitted, and he told the king the real reason.

"You are an evil man," said the king, "not to give credit to your teacher. When one gets good honey, one should not care what kind of trees it came from, and likewise when you get a great charm what does it matter if you got it from a brahman, a warrior, a merchant, or a servant. What difference does the birth of the teacher make if he has something priceless to offer!" And the angry king ordered the brahman banished from the kingdom until he recovered the charm.

The brahman returned to the chandala village and tried to gain the charm again by apologizing to his teacher, but the wise chandala knew the charm would never stay with the brahman, and so he sent him away. The dejected man withdrew into the woods and died.

In the above story the Buddha is portrayed as a man of low caste, which is not the usual practice. The story probably appealed to the early Buddhists because its message paralleled their claim that insight into religious truth had been gained by a non-brahman (the Buddha), who had undertaken to teach all who were sincere seekers, regardless of social status.

4
Monastic Values

When Aryan invaders, who called themselves "noblemen," came to India in the middle centuries of the second millennium B.C., they quickly encountered ascetic and mendicant holy men who affronted their pleasure- and world-oriented sacrificial religious system and beliefs. While the Aryan language, Sanskrit, has served as the vehicle for much Indian religious and philosophical thought, it is the ascetic goal of world renunciation which has provided the supreme end for most Indian religious traditions—Hindu, Buddhist, and other. The Aryans brought with them to India the notion of two basic life-stages, *student* and *householder*. To accommodate the ascetic values which they encountered in India, they added two additional stages—the partially withdrawn *forest dweller* (*vanaprastha*) and the full detached *recluse* (*sannyasin*). Some Aryan sages turned from sacrifices designed to gain material blessings to a pessimistic, cyclical view of the world and of humankind. That is, some of the upper classes adopted the values of India's native hermits.

Even the highly valued aims of the householder and the king

145

were superceded by the later Hindu lawbook encouragements to renounce the world and its enticements. Worldly success (*artha*), sexual gratification (*kama*), and proper adherence to one's duty (*dharma*) were proper aims for the householder who would live fully in the world, as has been reflected in many of the stories so far. But the new goals encouraged liberation (*moksha*) from the very same world of sensual enjoyment the previous stages uphold. In the stories that follow, the values that are extolled deal with proper detachment from worldly enticements and the development of mental and physical self-control. These are the general values of the monastic life, though their adherents may be solitary recluses, mendicant beggars, or fully ordained monks in a Buddhist or Hindu order. And, as we have seen in several stories, "monastic" values sometimes are adopted by laypersons as well.

While Buddhist teachings encourage young men (and sometimes women) to depart from the worldly life in their early years, Hindu traditions usually encourage a man to marry, have offspring, and live the life of a householder for many years before retiring into celibacy and self-control. The story "The Ascetic Who Visited Home" brings out the tension which exists between these two approaches to world-renunciation.

Whether the man takes up monastic life as a youth in the Buddhist fashion or later in life as in the Hindu fashion, the values of self-control, asceticism, detachment, and compassion are fundamental, as may be seen in the following stories.

SELF-CONTROL
Hindu Stories

One of the first steps toward detachment from the world's pleasures is to practice control over sensual desires. It is assumed that control of physical or sensual cravings is a foundation upon which later spiritual and mental gains can be built. Just as asceticism is the most extreme form of bodily restraint, so it is that lust and greed are the most feared enemies of self-control. Here is a delightful story of runaway greed in a jackal.

The Foolish Jackal

In a distant country there lived a hunter who existed on the flesh of the animals he killed. Very early one morning, the hunter shouldered his bow and arrows and set off for the woods to hunt. Soon he killed a deer with one shot from his bow, stripped the deer of its meat, and headed homeward. On his return journey the hunter descended a steep riverbank and came face to face with a huge boar wallowing in the mud with tusks uplifted. When the hunter turned to use another route, the boar ran and blocked his path.

Terrified, the hunter threw down the deer meat, grabbed a poison-tipped arrow, and placed it in his bow. The skillful hunter shot the boar through the neck. Though mortally wounded, the boar gave one last lunge and gored the hunter's stomach until his entrails fell out upon the ground. The bowman kneeled over dead as the boar succumbed to the poisoned arrow.

A lean and hungry jackal in search of food happened upon the bloody scene. When he saw the deer meat, the dead hunter, and the boar he said to himself, "Fate is kind to me today! It has given me all of this food so unexpectedly. I must eat it in such a way that I can live off this catch for a long time."

The jackal continued to ponder his find. "In order to make all of this food last, I will put the deer, the boar, and the hunter in a pile to be enjoyed later and first eat the cord with which the hunter's bow is strung." He took the bow string in his mouth to gnaw on the tough sinew, but when he had eaten through the bow cord, the bow snapped back to its natural position and, in the process, pierced the jackal's throat. He died on the spot.

The brahman's wife who tells this story recites its moral: "Always be thrifty, but do not be too thrifty. Because he was too thrifty, the jackal was killed by the bow." It seems that the moderation encouraged by Indian tales that warn against excessive greed, lust, or anger does not apply to positive attempts to control bodily or emotional tendencies. Extreme discipline of body or emotions is considered the aim in many Indian narratives. The tale of Jajali shows the extreme to which a compassionate act might be taken and yet be turned into destructive pride.

The Standing Ascetic

Jajali was an accomplished ascetic who could perform the severest austerities without flinching. He performed both morning and evening devotions and carefully tended the sacred fire as he devotedly studied the sacred texts. He lived in a woods unsheltered from the extremes of weather. In autumn he was exposed to the drenching monsoon rains, and in summer he endured the hot sun, unprotected by shade of any kind.

During one rainy season, Jajali's uncut hair became matted from the rain and strong winds. During that time, he had decided to fast while remaining motionless in one place. Therefore, Jajali stood in the forest as still as a wooden post according to his vow.

Out of compassion and with great restraint, Jajali stood im-

mobile while two Kulinga birds made a nest in his tangled hair. According to their pattern, the female bird laid her eggs in the nest and both birds enjoyed the comfort of their protected home. When the eggs had hatched, both birds brought food for their young ones to eat. Though time dragged on, Jajali was determined not to do injury to the creatures nesting in his hair, and he remained motionless.

In due time, the baby birds grew feathers, and the mother and father birds were proud of their handsome family. They all felt safe in their matted-hair home. The foremost of ascetics looked on as the young birds began to fly, leaving their nest for short excursions into the forest only to return to their nest each night. The young birds' development continued until they would leave their nest at daybreak and not return until dusk each day. After a while, the now mature birds would venture off and not return for five or six days. Still Jajali did not move. Only when the birds once left not to return for a whole month did Jajali finally move from his place in the forest.

Jajali then felt that he had carried out his vow of protection and patience. He washed himself in the river and built a sacrificial fire. Looking up at the heavens, he proclaimed, "I have won great merit!"

⚊⚊⚊

The longer story of Jajali's adventures (of which the nesting birds episode forms only a part) ends with praise for this accomplished saint's attitude of non-injury but also with chastisement for his excessive pride at his great feat of self-restraint. The storyteller interprets the bird episode allegorically as the deeds of a person, which come home to roost in the same manner as that in which they were given birth. So Jajali benefited from his act of kindness, but had to suffer embarrassment due to the prideful attachment he showed for his own feat. Even the control of one's body and senses may be turned into an act of attachment.

Buddhist Stories

In keeping with the middle path, Buddhist monks did not idealize the extremes of bodily mortification encouraged by many Indian ascetic groups. Rigid control of one's senses and emotions was permitted if harm of any kind was avoided. Nonetheless, self-control is for the Buddhists just one of many means toward the development of spiritual wisdom. Yet the heroes of many Buddhist stories exhibit strong self-control in order to accomplish their religious purposes. In the following story, a youth's Buddhist convictions lead him to amazing feats of self-control in order to avoid becoming king.

The Mute Prince

Once there was a just king of Banaras who had a harem full of wives but neither a son nor a daughter. He ordered his sixteen thousand wives to perform the traditional rituals for becoming pregnant, such as worshipping the moon and other appropriate deities, but with no success. The citizens begged the king to provide an heir to the throne, and he in turn asked his chief wife to pray especially hard. On the next full moon day she kept all the vows and spent the day thinking about her life, which had been virtuous. She then made this declaration: "If it be true that I have never broken any of the moral rules, may I conceive a son by the power of this truth." Her Act of Truth made the throne of Sakka heat up once more, and the god decided to help her. He went to the Future Buddha, who had been reborn in heaven after having spent several thousand years suffering in hell. The Future Buddha agreed to be reborn in the womb of the chief wife, and five hundred others from heaven were conceived in the other royal wives.

The baby was born to the chief wife ten lunar months later and named Temiya. His body showed all the signs of a great and wise person. His father adored him and often held the baby on his lap as he sat at court. The infant was thus exposed to the nature of kingship, and one day he listened to his father pronounce sentences upon criminals, such as one thousand lashes with a barbed whip, life in chains, and death by impalement. This experience caused the baby to recollect one of his past lives in which he had been a king who had imposed such punishments, and as a result he had suffered for thousands of years in hell! With that in mind young Temiya determined never to allow himself to become king.

A spirit who lived in the royal umbrella [the insignia of kingship in India] suggested to him that he escape the kingship by pretending to be deaf, dumb, and paralyzed, and he took the spirit's advice. At first the courtiers thought the heir apparent was merely melancholy, so they brought toys, but Prince Temiya did not react to them. They tested him by skipping his feedings, but he would not reach for them. When he was three they tried to get him interested in toy elephants, without success. When he was four they tried other foods.

When Temiya was five and still would not speak or move, the desperate king tried scaring him by setting fire to the building he was in, but if the courtiers had not grabbed the prince at the last minute he would have been burned to death. At six, the king turned an elephant loose near Temiya, but still he did not move. Serpents were tried when he was seven and eight, and then a more positive approach was tried. A party was given with jugglers and mimes, and the other children shouted with glee, but Temiya was still. They also tested him with loud noises, sword wielders, and insects, but he persisted. And when he was in his teens he did not respond when they brought beautiful girls before him.

Finally it was decided that the prince's body was inhabited by a goblin rather than a human, so the king ordered a servant to take Temiya to the burial ground the next morning, hit him with a spade, and bury him. Temiya's mother pleaded with him all

152

through the night, saying that she knew he could really speak and hear, but he ignored her tearful pleas.

As the servant dug the hole at the burial place, Temiya decided it was time to stop acting. He slowly flexed his limbs and walked to the servant and told the surprised man that he intended to go farther into the forest and become a hermit ascetic, now that he had escaped the kingship. Temiya was so persuasive about the ascetic life that the servant wanted to join him, but Temiya sent him back to the palace to explain to his mother that her son was alive but would not return.

The servant's bizarre tale spread quickly throughout the court and a huge crowd accompanied the king and queen as they rode out to the forest to persuade the prince to reconsider. The king begged, the queen touched his feet to honor him, and the citizens pleaded, but Temiya refused to become king. Temiya offered them leaves as food, and taught them the principles and advantages of the humble life of an ascetic. He was so effective as a spiritual teacher that hundreds of the courtiers and citizens and even the king himself left the worldly life. A large monastery was built, and all the new ascetics lived virtuously under Temiya's direction.

We turn from the larger-than-life story of Temiya's model self-control to a story about a woman whose self-control knows more realistic limits. The Buddha tells the following story as part of a lengthy instruction to his disciples on the necessity to train one's mind to the point that it is not disturbed even in adverse circumstances.

The Servant Who Tested Her Mistress

There was once a woman named Vedehika who was the head of a household in the city of Savatthi. She had the reputation of being very gentle and even-tempered. One day her female servant wondered if her mistress really had as much self-control as everyone thought. "After all," thought the servant, "my mistress does not need to get angry with me because I always get up early and do all the housework cheerfully." As a test, the servant slept a little late the next morning. When the mistress asked the reason, the servant said, "It's nothing." The mistress merely gave the servant a scolding glance.

The next day the servant overslept even more and again was unremorseful when questioned. This time the mistress scolded her quite a bit but maintained her self-control.

On the third morning the servant slept very late and when reprimanded, again said "It doesn't matter." "Indeed it does matter!" exploded the mistress, who seized the iron door bolt and hit the servant on the head with it.

The next day the servant showed the horrible gash on her head to all the neighbors, and the poor mistress was never again able to regain her good reputation, no matter how hard she tried.

The ability to be under control at all times, even when people offer constructive criticism or abuse you is very important, the Buddha concludes after telling this story about the woman who lost her control. Certainly, self-control is needed in all aspects of the religious life.

ASCETICISM
Hindu Stories

Of all the forms of self-control practiced in India and Asia, ascetic mortifications of the flesh are the most difficult for non-Asians to comprehend. The basis for asceticism (*tapas*) in India is the belief that great merit and power are generated by asceticism. The physical universe can be affected by such ascetic feats as fasting, exposing oneself to the elements, going without sleep, and meditating. We have seen many examples of the popular motif that the very seat of Indra, king of the gods, becomes hot by the heat created by an ascetic's practices.

Asceticism is sometimes recommended as a life-long practice, especially in the Jain religion of India, but in popular tales ascetic techniques are usually undertaken for a short period in order to achieve some specific, and often worldly, goal. Asceticism practiced for the acquisition of worldly rewards is thought virtually to compel the gods to grant the desired boons, due to the power of ascetic practice. We have already seen how Jajali's ascetic self-neglect was intended for spiritual gain. The two stories that follow give two more examples of ascetic practice undertaken for some specific worldly goal.

A Boon of Immortality

The demon king Hiranyakashipu wanted to be free from old age, disease, and the might of his enemies. In fact, Hiranyakashipu wanted to gain immortality and rule the whole universe—including the realm of Brahma, lord of creation. He considered the best way to achieve his desires to be the performance of severe austerities, and consequently, set off for the Mandara Valley. When he arrived in the auspicious valley, the demon king began his self-mastery by standing on his toes looking skyward while extending his arms high over his head. This awkward positioning of the body was hard to maintain, but the demon persisted in order to achieve his desired goals.

As Hiranyakashipu restrained his body, there shot forth from the matted hair on his head a bright light as intense as that of the sun itself. Both fire and smoke spread throughout the heavens, encompassing all the planets with the intense heat generated by the demon's austerities. The rivers and oceans were agitated, the earth quaked, and stars and planets fell from the sky. The whole universe was endangered by the demon's uncommon ascetic exercise.

The celestials abandoned their increasingly heated and uncomfortable realms and rushed to the abode of Brahma and said, "Oh Lord, master of the worlds, due to the intense heat resulting from Hiranyakashipu's austerities we are not able to reside on our celestial planets. Great god, please stop this danger which threatens our universe. Hiranyakashipu wishes to gain immortality and dethrone you as lord over all creation. But you are the master of the universe. All wealth and good fortune come from your auspicious reign, so please use whatever means you choose to rid us of this death-dealing threat."

Accompanied by an entourage of celestial sages, Brahma set off for the Mandara Valley, but when he came to the spot where Hiranyakashipu was said to be engaged in his ascetic feats, he could not see the demon. Due to the length of the austerities, Hiranyakashipu's body was covered with an anthill, grass, and bamboo twigs. Ants had devoured his fat, skin, flesh, and blood. The heavenly assembly led by Brahma was struck with wonder when they found the demon's body racked by physical torture yet emitting an intense heat.

Brahma said, "Son of a great sage, please get up and cease your austerities. You are now perfect in your ascetic practice and I give you my blessing. Ask of me whatever you wish and I will grant you that boon. I am astonished at your persistence and at your body's endurance. No saint previously born nor any yet to come could exhibit austerities as severe as yours. Who else could survive for one hundred celestial years without even one drink of water? With these feats, I certainly have been conquered by you. I am prepared to give you what you desire."

After speaking to Hiranyakashipu, Brahma sprinkled divine water from his water pot upon the remains of the demon's riddled body, and Hiranyakashipu arose from the anthill with a new body. As he stood up, Hiranyakashipu's appearance was that of a youth, strong armed with the might of a thunderbolt, and a complexion as bright as gold. Out of appreciation, Hiranyakashipu prostrated himself before Brahma and expressed his thankfulness.

The demon Hiranyakashipu desired a selfish end from his ascetic practice. He demanded and received the boon of not being able to be killed by man nor beast, in daylight or at night, and neither in a building nor outside. His hope was to rule the world eternally, but the demon's world rule was cut short by an incarnation of the god Vishnu. Taking the appearance of a half-lion and half-man creature (i.e., neither man nor beast), Vishnu ripped apart the evil demon in twilight (i.e., neither day nor night) on the porch of a temple (i.e., neither inside nor out). The ascetic boon of the demon had been granted and yet did not ensure the immortality he had desired.

A second tale which relates the use of asceticism for worldly gain ends on a more positive note since the warrior in question, Arjuna, desired a divine weapon to protect his people from their evil cousins.

Arjuna's Penance

Arjuna set off over nearly impassible mountains to find a place to perform his devotional penances. On the way, he fought with demons and thieves until at last he came to a grove of Ashoka trees along the banks of the Ganges River. Arjuna bathed in the Ganges, put on the robes of a sage, and began his devoted self-restraint. He set up a clay image of the god Shiva and stood in meditation before it. He continued his worship and fasting as he maintained his self-denying ascetic practices.

The heat generated by Arjuna's penances made the gods in heaven uncomfortable, and they went to Indra to seek relief. They said to Indra, "Someone is performing ascetic feats in the forest near the Ganges and we do not know whether it is a god, a sage, a fire, or the sun itself. Please remove this threat to our safety." Indra sent spies to test Arjuna's sincerity and resolve, but Arjuna continued his penances. Indra presented himself to Arjuna and commended him on his devoted persistence and awarded him the boon of error-free administration in his role as king.

Bouyed by the gracious boon of Indra, Arjuna renewed his ascetic practices with vigor. He practiced the control of breathing known to produce inner cleansing and calm. He recited for hours the five syllable prayer (*mantra*) praising Shiva as he stood before the clay image he had made. He stood on the sole of one foot and fixed one eye on the sun as he repeated the powerful prayer to Shiva. The gods in heaven were surprised at Arjuna's persistent self-negation and reported his mighty acts to Shiva.

Shiva decided to test Arjuna's devotion himself. Assuming the form of the hunter Kirata, Shiva went to the place of Arjuna's penance, arriving just as the demon Muka approached in the form of a gigantic boar. Seeing the boar rooting up mountains as he approached, Arjuna knew that this threatening animal was very likely just a demon's disguise. He abandoned his ascetic posture and unsheathed an arrow, which he let fly from his warrior's bow. At the very same instant, the disguised Shiva also shot at the boar to protect Arjuna, his devotee. Both Arjuna's and Shiva's arrows pierced the demon boar, killing it in its tracks. As the archers approached the boar to retrieve their spent arrows, an argument ensued as to which arrow killed the boar. Arjuna finally challenged the disguised Shiva to a hand-to-hand battle that would determine the owner of the disputed arrow.

Arjuna first fought Shiva's army and routed them in a short

time, receiving only minor injuries in the skirmish. Then the battle with Shiva (disguised as Kirata) began and Arjuna's task clearly became more difficult. The two warriors engaged each other with mighty blows and inflicted deep wounds. The tide began to turn when Kirata split Arjuna's weapons as well as his armor, leaving Arjuna standing naked and defenseless before him. Yet the fight raged on until Arjuna caught hold of Kirata's feet and flung him into the air. As Kirata flew up in the air his form changed into that of Shiva. Arjuna stood in disbelief to see that he had fought with the very god whom he had been worshipping.

Shiva reassured Arjuna that the whole fight had been a test of his resolve to continue his worship unrestricted by outside interference. Shiva furthermore granted Arjuna the goal of his long days of prayer and self-negation by giving him the divine weapon called Pashupata with the stipulation that it should be used just once, and only in the worst of predicaments. Arjuna's penance was over, and his boon had been won.

Buddhist Stories

Asceticism in Buddhist stories is seldom undertaken for the purpose of gaining a boon, as it is in the Hindu stories. Rather, *moderate* asceticism is to be a way of life for the Buddhist monk or nun. In the following story, however, we note that at least one immature Buddhist undertook the ascetic way of life in hopes of gaining beautiful women in heaven.

Asceticism Now, Nymphs Later!

A while after the Buddha attained enlightenment and had gathered around himself a large number of disciples, he agreed to visit his home city. While there, he came for alms to the house of his cousin, Prince Nanda, on the day of Nanda's marriage. The Bud-

159

dha approached Nanda and handed his almsbowl to him. Nanda followed the Buddha, expecting that at any moment the Buddha would take back the bowl, but he did not. Nanda followed him out of the house and through the village. Meanwhile the poor bride was informed of the strange happening and hurried off after Nanda, calling, "Come back, Lord, come back." Nanda could not bring himself to request that the Buddha carry his own almsbowl, so he carried it all the way to the park where Buddha was staying with his disciples. Once there, Buddha took the bowl and said, "Do you wish to become a monk?" Actually, Nanda wished to get married, but his respect for the Buddha was so great that he answered "Yes."

After Nanda had been a monk for a few days he complained to some of the other disciples that he wanted to return to the lay life and be reunited with his fiancée. The Buddha learned of his desire and took Nanda on a magical journey to heaven. There Nanda saw the five hundred celestial nymphs who serve the god Sakka's every need. The Buddha asked him which he found more attractive, his earthly fiancée or these five hundred nymphs. Nanda quickly replied, "My fiancée is much more attractive than the old monkey we saw on our journey here, but these pink-footed nymphs are that much more attractive still." Then the Buddha promised Nanda that if he would diligently follow the path of celibacy and monasticism, he would be rewarded in heaven with five hundred nymphs like Sakka's.

Nanda and Buddha returned to earth, and Nanda applied himself to meditation with renewed vigor. However, he was not respected by his fellow monks because his motivation was so base. They called him "the paid ascetic." By his long hours of meditation and solitude Nanda eventually experienced a mental transformation. After this breakthrough, Nanda came to the Buddha and said, "Lord, I now have gotten beyond the lust for women. I wish to free you from your promise of celestial nymphs. I no longer desire them." The Buddha responded that he knew the transformation had already occurred.

160

Nanda's fellow monks were not so quick to accept his change of heart, so the Buddha called them together and explained the situation. They then praised the Buddha for his clever approach to bringing Nanda into the fold of those who had gone beyond the lusts of the flesh.

The following story presents the more typical Buddhist response to the popular Indian notion that ascetic denials are undertaken for the sake of some material reward. We told the first part of the story of Ratthapala earlier under the title, "The Only-Child Who Left Home," and now we continue with the story of his return visit.

The Ascetic Who Visited Home

After Ratthapala had made great spiritual progress as a monk, he decided that it was proper for him to keep his promise to return to his parents. So he approached the Buddha, greeted him reverently, took a seat at one side, and said, "Lord, I wish to visit my parents, with your permission." The Buddha knew the advanced state of the disciple's mind and so readily agreed.

Ratthapala journeyed toward his home town and took up residence at the outskirts in a park where monks often stayed. Early one morning at the proper time for begging he went to his parents' home for alms. His father happened to be in front of the house but did not recognize his son. The father remarked to his wife that the shaved, saffron-robed monk out front must be from the same sect as their son, but they were still bitter about losing their son and so did not go out to put anything in the monk's almsbowl.

Meanwhile Ratthapala continued to stand there silently, as Buddhist monks must do, because he had been neither fed nor dismissed. A slave girl came outside to throw away some day old porridge, and Ratthapala said to her, "If you are just going to throw that away, why not put it in my bowl?" She did, and recognizing his voice she went to tell his mother, who in turn told her husband. Ratthapala's father hurried to him and said, "You're not eating cold leftovers, are you? Come back to your home and the servants will prepare a nice, hot meal." "There is no such thing as 'home' for one who has gone forth from home, and besides I have finished eating for today," Ratthapala answered in a detached way.

Eventually Ratthapala consented to eat the next day's meal at his parents' home. His father ordered his kitchen servants to prepare the most sumptuous meal and the other servants to gather all the family's jewels and other valuables into piles in the living room. He ordered his daughter-in-laws to dress in their sexiest clothing and jewels the next day, to remind their husband of the pleasures of the secular life.

When Ratthapala arrived and took his seat, his father explained which pile of valuables was his inheritance from his great grandfather, which from his maternal uncle, and so forth. After pointing all this out, he said, "Son, it is possible to live here rich and happy, while also performing the good works which a layman can do to earn lots of merit." "If you want my advice, householder," the monk said to his father, "you should load all this gold and glitter into wagons and go dump it in the Ganges River! Why? Because wealth such as this will only be a cause of suffering for you."

This left his father speechless, giving his former wives a chance to try their powers of persuasion. They approached him and touched his feet to honor him and asked, "What kind of celestial nymphs do you expect to win from your celibacy?" He quickly replied, "Sisters, we do not live the celibate life for the sake of nymphs." " 'Sisters'? Our husband called us 'Sisters,' " they sobbed to each other in disbelief.

Ratthapala turned to his father and said, "If you are going to offer food, please get on with it and stop harassing me." So the father personally offered food to the monk, who ate his fill and went back to the park.

~~~~~~

On a subsequent day the king approached Ratthapala in the park and said that he knew of only four reasons for departing the worldly life, and each was a kind of loss: loss of youth (i.e., senility), of health, of wealth, and of friends and loved ones. But why had Ratthapala left home, the king wondered, since he had suffered none of the four losses? Ratthapala explained to the king that he left the worldly life because he accepted the teaching of the Buddha, with its four insights into the nature of the world: the world passes away, brings dissatisfaction, is not subject to one's will, and is a servant of craving.

It is for such reasons as Ratthapala cited that so many Hindu and Buddhist stories such as the following teach that the wise person is detached from the world.

DETACHMENT
Hindu Stories

The goal of self-control in general and asceticism in particular is detachment from worldly enticements. According to Indian reasoning, if the world and our life in it are merely repeated images of an endless world cycle (*samsara*), then the ultimate spiritual achievement is liberation (*moksha*) from that world of suffering and rebirth. Detachment is more a frame of mind, an attitude of non-dependence, than a proclamation of physical and social separation from the world. Still, many in India who renounce the world do so by leaving family, friends, vocation, and home comforts to wander about living only on what can be begged.

The supreme test of people's claim to detachment from the world is their response to threats against their own lives, according to most Hindu and Buddhist folklore. To be unconcerned with one's own death is the ultimate expression of detachment. In the tale that follows, a young boy teaches his parents and the king this lesson.

The Boy Who Laughed at Death

Adjusting his position on the king's shoulder, the goblin once again posed a riddle for King Vikram:

"Once in a distant city there lived a king named Chandravaloka and his queen, Indumati. Together the king and queen enjoyed all the pleasures of life that wealth brings. However, one day the king lost his property in a gambling match and, despondent, mounted his horse and rode deep into a great forest. Tired and thirsty, the king stopped at the edge of a lake for a drink and lay down on the bank for a rest. Looking off in the distance, the king saw the hermitage of a sage.

"As the king approached the hermitage, he was struck with the beauty of a young woman, the sage's daughter, who greeted him as an honored guest. He was enraptured by the young woman and asked her, 'What causes a woman of such beauty as yourself to dwell in this dark forest? Do you have a loved one here?' The girl perceived the king's desires and responded, 'Dear king, you must hide in the forest since my father will soon return. Your desires will be met if you are patient.'

"When the sage returned to his hermitage, he observed that his daughter was acting in an unusual manner and asked her what was disturbing her. The young woman told of the king's visit and of their immediate attraction for each other. The sage gave his permission for the king to marry his daughter, and the young woman called out for the king to come out of hiding. The sage greeted the king and welcomed him as an appropriate husband for his daughter.

"After the king expressed his respect for the sage, he departed for his own country with his new-found love. En route they stopped to spend a night under a banyan tree. During the night, a demon appeared and threatened the king, 'You will be my meal today.' Discovering his visitor to be a demon, the king bargained, 'Let me go and I will give you a human sacrifice.' The demon responded, 'I shall name the offering I desire,' and the king agreed. The demon continued, 'You must provide a young boy as an offering for me.' 'In what way must the offering be conducted?' the king asked. The demon replied, 'The boy must willingly accept his own death as his mother holds his feet and you yourself cut off his head. Only then will I be satisfied.' The king consented to the conditions laid down by the demon and departed quickly for familiar country.

"Though the king sought diligently, he could find no young boy willing to meet the demon's demands. Then one day a young boy said to his parents, 'Father, give me as an offering to ensure good fortune for our king.' The boy's parents tried to dissuade him but the boy responded, 'If you do not permit me to be an offering, I will kill myself anyway. If I die, what does it matter? But if the king dies, everyone will perish. My duty to the king demands this action, how can it be wrong?' Taking his parents by the hand, the boy went off to see the king and offer himself as his substitute.

"The king, the parents and the young boy went off to the demon's haunt in the forest. When they arrived at the spot of his encounter with the demon, the king proceeded to sacrifice the boy according to his instructions. The king said to the boy, 'God-like one, call upon your household deity to protect you.' At these words the boy began to laugh uncontrollably. Knowing the past, present, and future, the demon laughed with the boy and refused him as a sacrifice."

The goblin then asked King Vikram, "Why did the boy and the demon laugh?" Vikram answered, "Listen goblin, the young boy reflected upon his plight with these thoughts, 'My mother and father hold my feet and hair; the king holds his sword ready to cut off my head; yet the king says, "Call upon your household deity." ' That is why the boy and demon laughed. At such a time of misfortune, who could protect the boy? That is why the demon sent home the wise and detached boy."

~~~~

The boy could not help laughing at the persistent attachment to life evidenced by his parents and king who—even at the moment of death—refused to accept the boy's death. Their attachment was simply funny from his detached perspective.

The following is an allegorical Indian story that shows how persistent human attachment to transitory life really is.

The Well of Life

A certain brahman who lived in this world wandered into a deep dark forest that was filled with ferocious wild animals. The forest was populated with lions, bull elephants, and other animals that roared incessantly. It was so terrifying that even the god of death, Yama, would cringe at entering this malevolent realm. Realizing he was lost, the brahman became very alarmed and began to run in circles hoping to find the way out. Attempting to elude the frightening creatures which were all around, the panicked man ran deeper into the forest. Still, he could not rid himself of his pursuers.

The brahman looked up and saw that the forest was surrounded by a net held by a huge woman with outstretched arms. Serpents with five heads also encompassed the forest and were so tall that their heads reached nearly up to the heavens. In a clearing, there was a deep pit covered with creeping vines and underbrush. As the brahman ran frantically through the forest pursued by a wild elephant, he stumbled into the open pit and became lodged halfway down the hole in the vines that grew over it.

As the brahman hung upside down, tangled in the vines, he

166

saw a huge serpent at the bottom of the hole. Looking up, he saw an elephant at the top of the hole. The dark-skinned elephant had six faces and twelve feet and seemed intent on maintaining its vigil at the mouth of the hole. In the vines that held the brahman, bees had built hives filled with honey. These hives dripped honey near him, and he reached out to catch the sweet nectar in his mouth as he hung there. The more honey the brahman ate, the more he wanted; his thirst could not be quenched. Meanwhile, black and white rats gnawed away at the roots of the vines which held him. With elephant above, serpent below, bees buzzing all around, and rats gnawing at his life-support, the brahman continued to reach out for more honey.

The story of the brahman in the pit is explained by the storyteller as an allegory of life itself. The inaccessible forest is really the limited sphere of one's life. The woman who holds a net over the forest is likened to the aging process which takes youth and vigor from the body. The beasts of the forest are the diseases that threaten every life, and the serpent at the bottom of the well is Time, the destroyer of all living beings. The creeping vines are the desires that entangle every person. The six-faced elephant with twelve feet represents the months of the year, and the white and black rats symbolize the days and nights. The honey represents the pleasures of life, and the story very simply shows the persistence of human attachment to life's pleasures in the face of innumerable dangers and inevitable death. The tragedy of life is that people continue to long for transient pleasures even until life's end. This is the nature of real attachment! This also is the nature of the transient world of rebirth (*samsara*).

Buddhist Stories

Detachment is one of the favorite themes of Buddhist story-tellers. Many stories, for example, deal with the wisdom of not grieving unduly at the death of a loved one. The stories teach that all people, indeed all things, pass away sooner or later, so the wise person does not become overly attached to them. Buddhists have never understood this to mean that close personal relationships should not be formed. Rather, one is supposed to keep always in mind the changing nature of things, the ever present possibility of separation from relatives, friends, or possessions. The first Buddhist story describes an advanced monk's extreme detachment from women. The important Buddhist commentator Buddhaghosa told this story to illustrate the way the detached person is not disturbed by the general appearance of other people or things.

The Man Who Didn't Notice Women

Once the senior monk named Mahatissa was going toward a town to get alms. That same morning a beautiful woman in the town had a bad quarrel with her husband and became so angry at him that she dressed up in her most seductive clothes and left home, looking like a heavenly nymph. As she traveled away from town she noticed Mahatissa coming toward her, gazing at the ground as Buddhist monks do when going for alms. To get even with her husband, she decided to flirt with the monk, so as she came near to him she began to giggle teasingly and then smiled as he looked up. The monk saw her foul teeth, and then continued on his way, reflecting upon the foulness of bodies—which deepened his spiritual insight.

A little later the woman's husband came along the road and asked Mahatissa if he had seen a beautiful young woman pass that way. The old monk replied, "Some bones passed this way, but I did not notice if they were male or female."

⟋⟍

It is easy to see that attachment to humans may lead to grief, but the Buddhist teaching goes beyond that to say that attachment to anything is problematic, for everything that has arisen will pass away. This includes even the seemingly timeless landmarks of India such as the sacred rivers and mountains, as the Buddha taught his monks by means of the following account of the destruction of the current world. (In traditional Indian cosmology the world is periodically destroyed, only to be created again after several thousand years.)

The Destruction of the World

Once when the Buddha was staying in a park near the city of Vesali he instructed his disciples in the value of being detached from all things in the world. He said, "Monks, all things which have been put together are impermanent and unstable. Therefore, be free from them."

The Buddha went on to say, "There will come a time when a drought lasting thousands of years will dry up the earth. Therefore, be free.

"Then, monks, a second sun will appear in the sky and the streams and small lakes will dry up. Therefore, be free.

"After another extremely long time, a third sun will appear, making the earth so hot that even the great rivers such as the Ganges will dry up and pass away. Therefore, be free.

"Again, a fourth sun will appear and the intense heat will dry up the large lakes. Therefore, be free.

"After another long period of time a fifth sun will appear and the oceans will begin to shrink and shrink until they are no bigger than the water that forms in a cow's hoofprints after a rain. Therefore, be free.

"Eventually a sixth sun will appear and there will be nothing left unscorched except the great mountains, but even they will emit smoke like a potter's oven. Therefore, be free.

"With the appearance of a seventh sun, the mountains will burn up, even Sineru, the king of all mountains. They will burn so hot that not even a cinder will be left. Monks, all things which have been put together are impermanent and unstable. Therefore, be free from them."

The Buddhist teaching that all things are impermanent and not worthy of ultimate attachment extends even to the Buddhist doctrine (*dharma*) itself. Buddha once made this point by a parable of the raft, which subsequently became a Buddhist favorite. The Buddha described a traveling man who came to a wide, deep river. To cross it he constructed a raft out of grass and brush. Once he had crossed over to the other side, he was so grateful to the raft that he put it on his back and carried it the rest of the way! The Buddha then encouraged his disciples not to make that same mistake, even with his teachings which should be used only as long as they are helpful.

Our final group of stories is about the compassion that should go hand in hand with detachment.

COMPASSION
Hindu Stories

The Hindu notion of detachment as the ultimate spiritual goal and attitude is reflected in the folktales which also show compassion to be a desirable trait for those who live and work in the world. The first *Panchatantra* tale advises compassion as a disposition beneficial to all kings.

The Dove and the Mouse

There was in the south a city named Mahilaropya. Near that city was a huge tree with many branches in which birds from the countryside would spend the night. One such bird, a crow named Lightwing, one day saw a fowler set a trap under the tree. The hunter placed his net upon the ground and sprinkled corn around as bait, and then hid behind a bush not far away.

In a short while, a dove king named Brightneck spotted the kernels of corn beneath the tree while flying above the tree with his flock. Brightwing unsuspectingly led his covey into the trap as he flew down to enjoy the tempting grain. The hunter rushed forward with club in hand as soon as he saw the doves caught in his net. The doves began flying in all directions trying to escape when their leader, Brightneck, said to them, "A disaster of great magnitude has fallen upon us and the only means to safety in such a case is for all of us to work together. We must all fly together in the same direction if we expect to carry off this net."

Hearing the sage advice of their leader, the doves all followed Brightneck's lead and the whole covey flew up in the air taking the net with them. When the approaching hunter saw his catch and his only net rising into the sky he said to himself, "This is impossible. Whoever heard of birds flying off with a fowler's net! To be sure, as long as that covey flies together, it can lift up the net. But as soon as the birds begin to disagree and argue, they will fall into my lap." The hunter ran along under the doves waiting for dissention to provide his meal.

When Brightneck saw the hunter following under the net, he encouraged his flock to go faster and instructed them to continue to fly as one. Lightwing, the crow, had been watching all of this and flew off after the doves to see what their fate would

172

be. Brightneck, realizing the fowler's strategy, said to his doves, "We must fly up even higher and travel over rugged country in order to lose that hunter who would take our lives." So the birds flew up even higher and crossed a mountain peak. When his daily catch and his net disappeared over a mountain, the fowler gave up hope and returned sadly to his home.

After the hunter turned back, Brightneck also had his flock return to Mahilaropya to the den of a friend of his, Goldy the mouse. Alighting near the mouse's hole, Brightneck called out, "Friend Goldy, please come and help us." Goldy was surprised and pleased to hear his friend's voice and rushed out to greet Brightwing. But when he saw the net he asked, "My friend, what is the meaning of this fate of yours?" Brightwing responded, "Indeed! You are an intelligent being, Goldy. You know that whenever, whatever, and by whatsoever means a person does a deed, good or evil, his action returns to him in like form by the hand of fate." Goldy agreed, "The same bird whose eyes can pick out a bit of meat upon the ground from hundreds of yards up in the sky fails to see a hunter's net at his feet when fate's time arrives."

Having assessed his friend's plight, Goldy began to chew off the net cords that surrounded Brightneck. Brightneck said, "Friend Goldy, cut first the cords from around my flock, and then attend to me." When Brightneck had insisted a second and then a third time, Goldy said impatiently, "My friend, why do you insist on aiding others in distress before you yourself are freed?" Brightneck responded, "Goldy, do not be angry. All of these doves about me have forsaken other leaders and have trusted me. Is it not right for me to ensure their safety? You should cut their restricting cords first in case your jaws become too tired to finish their task and some of my flock remains trapped while I am freed."

When Goldy heard his friend speak with such compassion, the mouse responded, "You have passed your trial of leadership. Because you have shown compassion to your followers and were

173

willing to share an unhappy fate with them, you have demonstrated the one quality which makes you fit to rule over the whole universe." So speaking, Goldy cut all the net's cords and freed all the doves. Brightneck expressed his appreciation and flew off with his flock of doves to their home.

Though detached compassion makes one fit "to rule the whole universe" according to Goldy, compassion arising from attachment can stand in the path of a person who is trying to renounce that very universe. This is the idea conveyed by the following tale of Bharata.

The Ascetic and the Deer

The sagely king Bharata performed his usual morning duties beside the Gandaki River. Just as Bharata sat down on the river bank to say his morning prayers, a pregnant black doe came down to the river to get a drink. While the doe was satisfying her thirst, a lion hunting close-by emitted a terrific roar. The frightened doe leaped into the river and, due to her fright, gave birth there. In her misfortune and fright, the does crawled out of the river and into a cave where she died.

Bharata too had been disturbed from his prayers by the lion's roar and had seen the mother deer's misfortune. Knowing the newborn deer which was floating down the stream to be motherless, Bharata stepped into the stream and rescued the fawn, then started back to his hermitage with the deer under his arm.

Although his spiritual duties were numerous, Bharata found time to care for the fawn. Day after day Bharata's affection for the fawn grew as he continued to provide grass and water for its nourishment. Bharata protected the fawn from the wild animals of the forest, and provided reassuring scratches and pats when it became nervous. Bharata became more and more attached to the

174

young deer as the occasions of fondling or an affectionate kiss multiplied. In the process of showing compassion to the motherless fawn, Bharata finally forgot his spiritual duties and practices and the spiritual advancement that was their goal.

Bharata thought to himself, "Alas, this helpless fawn which has lost its relatives, has come to me as a representative of god himself to be protected. I am its mother and father, and it trusts me as its friend. It would be selfish to abandon it even though it is disturbing my usual schedule of prayers and exercises. Even one who has renounced the world and taken those vows certainly must feel compassion for other suffering beings."

Bharata laid down with the fawn, took walks with it, ate with it, and bathed with it. Whenever the sage entered the forest to collect tender grass, flowers, roots, or water for the fawn, he would take his youthful pet with him. Together they played and worked. Bharata would often take the deer on his shoulders when on a walk, or on his lap when they were resting, or on his chest when they would sleep. Bharata's heart was filled with love for the deer he had rescued.

As time passed, Bharata became so attached to the deer that he was filled with anxiety when he was separated from it for a short while. Bharata would fantasize about wild creatures attacking the deer and would begin to blame himself for not being a better protector. So it was that Bharata became completely obsessed with caring for the deer until all his waking and dreaming moments were occupied with thoughts of the deer and its safety.

When Bharata was near death, he saw the deer sitting by his side exactly like a son lamenting his father's death. As death's veil was spread across Bharata's vision, his mind was fully engrossed with thoughts of the deer and, as a result, he acquired the form of a deer in his new birth! However, one thing separated Bharata from other deer. Although he had lost his human body and had received the body of a deer, Bharata retained his memory of his past life as a king, ascetic, and protector of the motherless fawn.

Remembering his past life, Bharata began to lament, "What misfortune I have brought upon myself. I have fallen from the path of the self-realized renouncers. I gave up my wife, family, and kingdom to seek eternal peace in the forest and to become detached from transitory affections and attachments. Instead, I became attached to a deer! Now I have obtained the body of a deer and have fallen far from my devotional practices." Thinking this way, Bharata left his deer family and went off to a forest hermitage to resume his devotional and ascetic practices.

Buddhist Stories

The Buddhas of past eras and the Buddhas of the future will be known for their compassion, as was Gautama, the Buddha for our era. The following story gives one of the many reasons why one title for a Buddha is "The Compassionate One."

Tend the Sick

Once the Buddha and his traveling assistant, Ananda, were touring a monastery when they came upon a very sick man who was lying in his own excrement. "What is the matter, monk?" the Buddha asked. "I have very bad dysentery, Lord," the sick man replied.

"Why are the other monks neglecting you?" the Buddha inquired. The weak and helpless monk answered, "Because they consider me useless." The Buddha immediately sent Ananda off for water, and when he brought some, the Buddha poured the water while Ananda washed the man. Then they moved him to a clean bed.

When they had finished, the Buddha called a meeting of the monks of that monastery and asked them why they had not tended to the needs of their brother. They confessed it was because the monk was useless to the Order. The patient Buddha then said, "Brothers if you do not take care of each other, who will, for you have left your parents and relatives behind? Brothers, if you wish to tend me, tend the sick."

And the Buddha pronounced that from that time on the failure to tend to the needs of sick brothers would be considered an offense against the monks' disciplinary vows.

~

When he was eighty years old and becoming weak of body, the Buddha contracted a severe case of dysentery himself. As he lay dying, he did a very compassionate thing, according to the following story.

The Dying Buddha's Compassion

The Buddha and some of his disciples traveled to Pava, where they stayed at a grove of trees owned by a metalsmith named Chunda. Chunda was very pleased to learn that the venerable Buddha was staying on his property. He went out to the Buddha and asked permission to offer a meal for the monks the next morning.

The meal Chunda offered included several dishes, including one called Sukara [the identity of which is not certain]. The Buddha intuited that the Sukara was spoiled but did not want to say so in front of Chunda. Instead the Buddha said, "Chunda, serve that Sukara only to me, for I intuit that in all the world only a Buddha can properly digest it, and bury whatever is left over in the ground." In this way the other monks were spared the obligation of eating the bad food, and Chunda's pleasure at providing hospitality for the Buddha and his monks was not diminished. After the Buddha had eaten a generous amount of the Sukara and the monks had eaten the rice curries and other cakes,

177

the Buddha instructed Chunda in religious matters and then left with his monks.

Later the Buddha became quite ill with dysentery. He had a terrible thirst and asked for water from a nearby stream. His attendant, Ananda, protested because the stream had recently been muddied by the passage of five hundred oxcarts. But the Buddha insisted on having the water, and when Ananda drew some from the stream it miraculously became clear.

Still later the Buddha laid down on his side and there, in his weakened state and near death, he realized in his compassion that after his death some of the monks might blame his death upon Chunda. So he said, "Ananda, if anyone begins to say, 'This is an evil thing that Chunda did,' you correct them by quoting me as saying, 'This is a good thing that Chunda did for it is a great honor to have provided the last meal for a Buddha.' Tell Chunda and the others that his good deed has won him a great reward in heaven." Not long after that, the final nirvana of the Buddha occurred. As he lay dying the angels gathered around him and the trees rained down blossoms.

We can see in this story the Indian ideal of a person who is so detached that he does not fear death yet so compassionate that he thinks of others even in violent illness and death.

One of the most important Buddhist stories about compassion describes the many vows taken by a Buddhist who undertook to become a Buddha. In one of his vows he promised not to enter into paradise unless he could bring all beings with him. According to his followers, the man did progress to enlightenment, under the name Buddha Amida, and he now reigns over a great and splendid paradise in the West to which all beings who have faith in him can go. It would have been possible for him to simply enjoy the bliss of the nirvana he had won, but instead he chose out of compassion to provide the possibility of a happy afterlife for all creatures. Because of his great compassion, and in the hope of

being admitted into the Western Paradise, millions of Mahayana Buddhists through the ages have prayed, "Homage to Amida Buddha."

In this chapter we have focused on the spiritual values of self-control, asceticism, detachment, and compassion which are sometimes relevant to Buddhist and Hindu laymen and are fundamental to monks. The stories themselves often illustrate more than one of these values, which are interdependent. For example, ascetics need self-control, and yet detachment must be offset by compassion.

Conclusion

We have retold some of the thousands of Hindu and Buddhist stories of life. On one level, these stories both entertain and instruct the listeners on how life should be lived. Many of the stories have told of rather extreme cases of virtue, and these have provided *models for* the proper fulfillment of one's life role—as wife, husband, king, monk. Other stories have offered *images of* improper behavior, clearly implying that one should behave in the opposite manner. Many stories, of course, provide both model functions in their complexities of plot and characters.

The stories have usually included a sanction, a reward or punishment for good or bad moral action. For their evil deeds, our characters have experienced such punishments as rebirth in hell, in an animal body, or as a miserable ghost. For good deeds, there have been pleasant rebirths in heaven or on earth as a rich or wise human. The stories take for granted the belief in rebirth and in the moral force (*karma*), which punishes evil and rewards goodness.

A strong belief in the interconnectedness of humans, animals, nature, and the divine undergirds Indian story traditions. Acts of ascetic self-control are said to have generated great amounts of psychic power, which, in turn, can be used to work miracles or to gain spiritual wisdom. All nature is bountiful, according to several of the stories, when humans (whether kings or commoners) perform their appointed tasks well. And the reverse is true also.

Besides the classical religious stories we have drawn upon, there are many other sources of instruction about life in the Indian tradition, some of which run counter to the ascetic bent of the stories in this volume. For example, there are popular proverbs that extoll the acquisition of wealth, political power, or progeny. And there are didactic manuals, such as the famous *Kamasutra*, that attempt to enhance erotic pleasures within certain bounds. Dramas, both classical and modern, have also played a large role in shaping Indian moral values, as have rituals and festivals which instruct and motivate. And, of course, there are many stories that were either too regional or too modern to be included in our selection. Furthermore, Muslim, Jain, Sikh, and Christian stories would also need to be included to develop a total picture of Indian stories of life.

The Buddhist and Hindu stories of our collection share certain moral presuppositions and content common to all Indian spirituality. Yet, there are obvious differences, which are related to Gautama Buddha's attempt to reform certain tenets of Hinduism as it existed in the sixth century B.C. Buddha's insistence upon non-violence led him to reject animal sacrifice, not to mention widow sacrifice (i.e., *sati*). So the Hindu story of "The Goddess Who Drank Blood," which supports the practice of sacrificing animals to Kali, contrasts with the Buddhist story of "The Goat Who Laughed and Cried," which condemns even the violence involved in a religious sacrifice. Buddha's rejection of sacrificial rituals parallels his rejection of caste and the superior role of the priestly brahman class. In place of the stories about good or bad brahmans, the Buddhists told stories about pious and learned monks. We note that there are very few stories portraying evil monks, though Hindu stories of evil brahmans abound.

We also note that in the Buddhist stories, young men and women are encouraged to depart from the worldly life even before they have married and had sons, whereas in classical Hinduism a man was encouraged to take the *sannyasi* vows of a holy man late in life, after living the life of a householder and siring sons. Therefore, Hindu stories such as "A Handful of Rice" reveal an appreciation for this world when placed in a context of devotion, which the Buddha's negative assessment could not permit. In our Buddhist stories, those who practice asceticism usually do so for the sake of winning wisdom and eventually the state of ultimate bliss, nirvana. The pursuit of wisdom is also one reason for a Hindu to practice asceticism, but in our stories, the Hindu heroes sometimes use their ascetic power for rather worldly goals, such as marrying a beautiful princess in the case of Narada, the monkey-faced suitor.

Running through the Buddhist stories is the teaching that the monastic Order made up of all classes is worthy of financial and other support, whereas the Hindu stories call for allegiance to the birth/class system headed by the brahmans. So it is that King Vikram answers the goblin that only a warrior is a suitable husband for a woman of the warrior class.

Stories such as those represented in our collection have enjoyed a wide exposure in India. For example, many of our stories have been painted or carved on temple walls. Buddhist temples typically have illustrations from the *Jataka* stories and scenes from the life of the Buddha painted on the walls surrounding the central shrine room. In many temples, several *Jatakas* and the major scenes from Buddha's life come into view as one circumambulates the shrine room. The beautiful cave paintings at Ajanta and the stone-carved gateways around the stupa at Sanchi are outstanding examples of Buddhist story art. The same point may be made of Hindu temple art. Scenes from the *Ramayana* or *Mahabharata* are carved in layered bands of stone on Hindu temples

185

and serve as visual reminders of these influential stories. Likewise, episodes from the life of Krishna provide the subject matter of hundreds of miniature paintings.

Hindu and Buddhist stories have also been incorporated into festivals, which give them annual exposure. The most important festival of the Buddhist year is held at the last full moon before the beginning of the rainy season and celebrates the birth, enlightenment, and death (*parinirvana*) of the Buddha. The festival of the setting of the wheel in motion follows shortly thereafter. Hindu festivals usually parade through the streets an image of the deity being honored and include a retelling, often in dramatic form, of the life story of that god or goddess. For example, the birthday of the god Krishna (August/September) occasions festive depictions all over India of episodes from his life story (especially those linked to his ornery childhood).

Traveling theatrical groups have done their share in keeping alive the classical stories of India. The epic of Rama and Sita, a part of which we have retold, has long been a favorite among Indians of all religious persuasions. So too the classical dance traditions rely upon Hindu myths and epics for most of their subject matter.

Though Buddhism's influence waned in India in the early centuries of this era, it was the *Jatakas* and other such stories which often captured the imagination of new converts in Southeast Asia, China, and Japan. Meanwhile, the Buddhist temples and stupas of India continue as silent witnesses to this vital story tradition which has enjoyed a resurgence among the poor of India in the twentieth century.

Thus, through the centuries, the stories that have been so vital a part of life in India have been transmitted from generation to generation through temple art, priests, professional actors, festival dancers, and, perhaps most importantly, by parents and grandparents in the extended family setting. It is some sense of the vitality and impact of these narrative traditions that we have sought to convey in this small sampling of India's rich story lore.

186

Story Sources

Our stories are translated or retold from the following sources. English titles follow original language titles where appropriate.

Stories	Sources
Chapter 1	
"The Brahman in the Graveyard"	*Vetālapañcaviṁśati* ("Twenty-five Tales of the Goblin," Jambhaladatta's version), Story no. 2
"Good King Nala's Downfall"	*Mahābhārata*, III. 52-79
"The Wisdom of a Child"	*Jātaka*, Story no. 446
"The Carpenter's Wife"	*Pañchatantra*, Book III, Story no. 8
"Savatri and the God of Death"	*Mahābhārata*, III. 291-99
"The Radiant Sambula"	*Jātaka*, Story no. 519
"The Queen Who Cried Rape"	*Jātaka*, Story no. 120
"The Prostitute Who Lost Her Charm"	*Dhammapadaṭṭhakathā* ("Buddhist Legends"), Book XI, Story no. 2
"A Goddess Is Born"	*Śiva Purāṇa*, 2.2.13-14
"A Journey into Hell"	*Mahābhārata*, XVIII. 1-3
"How a King Learned To Care for Parents"	*Jātaka*, Story no. 540
"The Only-Child Who Left Home"	*Majjhima-nikāya* ("The Middle Length Sayings"), Sutra no. 82
Chapter 2	
"The Serpent with One Hundred Heads"	*Bhāgavata Purāṇa*, X. 15

187

Chapter 3

189

Selected Bibliography

I. Resources for the Study of Myth and Folklore

Cohen, Percey. "Theories of Myth." *Man* 4:337-53. 1969. A good overview and brief analysis of basic approaches (psychological, social, etc.) used to study myth.

Crim, Keith, ed. *Abingdon Dictionary of Living Religions*. Nashville: Abingdon Press, 1981. An alphabetical reference of high quality which includes the primary characters of Hindu and Buddhist myths, fables, and other stories.

de Carvalho-Neto, Paulo. *Folklore and Psychoanalysis*. Trans. by J. M. P. Wilson. Coral Gables: University of Miami Press, 1968. A Jungian approach to folklore and mythology.

Dundes, Alan, ed. *The Study of Folklore*. Englewood Cliffs: Prentice-Hall, 1965. A collection of wide-ranging essays which treat topics as varied as American fairy tales and ancient solar myths.

Eliade, Mircea. *Myth and Reality*. Trans. by W. R. Trask. New York: Harper & Row, 1963. The first four chapters relate a descriptive and functional definition of myth which takes seriously its experiential dimensions.

Farquhar, John N. *Outline of the Religious Literature of India*. New Delhi: Motilal Banarsidass, 1967 (reprint). An old but still useful survey of Indian literature.

191

Frankfort, Henri. "Myth and Reality." In *Before Philosophy*, ed. by H. Frankfort *et. al.*, pp. 11-36. Baltimore: Pelican Book, 1949. An explanation of myth as a type of "primitive" thinking called "mytho-poeic" which is said to be pre-logical and pre-scientific.

Freud, Sigmund. *The Future of an Illusion*. New York: Anchor Books, 1964. Freud's generalized argument that religious belief is analogous to childhood neurosis and, therefore, myths are "the fairy tales" of religion.

Geertz, Clifford. "Religion as a Symbol System." In *Reader in Comparative Religion*, ed. by William A. Lessa and Evon Z. Vogt, pp. 167-78. 3rd ed. New York: Harper & Row, 1965. An explication of religion as a complex and self-validating symbol system in which myths are vehicles of a religious world view.

Jacobs, Melville, and John Greenway, eds. *The Anthropologist Looks at Myth*. Austin: University of Texas Press, 1966. A useful collection of essays that analyze myth and folklore from both social and psychological perspectives.

Jung, Carl. *The Archetypes and the Collective Unconscious*. Trans. by R. F. C. Hull. Vol. 9, Part 1 of *Collected Works*. New York: Pantheon Books, 1953-79. The presentation by Jung of his controversial claim that all persons share the potentiality for certain basic symbolic forms ("archetypes") which occur in dreams, myths, and visions.

———. *Psyche and Symbol*. New York: Doubleday, 1958. A selection from the writings of Jung with emphasis on symbols, archetypes, and the unconscious.

Leach, Edmund. *Claude Lévi-Strauss*. New York: Viking Press, 1970. A good introduction to the life and thought of Lévi-Strauss, but an especially clear presentation of his structural approach to myth.

Lévi-Strauss, Claude. "The Story of Asdiwal." In *The Structural Study of Myth and Totemism*, ed. by Edmund Leach, pp. 1-47. London: Tavistock Publications, 1967. A good example of structuralism applied to a set of variants of one myth, in this case belonging to a native American tribe.

———. "The Structural Study of Myth." In *Reader in Comparative Religion*, ed. by William A. Lessa and Evon Z. Vogt, pp. 289-302. 3rd ed. New York: Harper & Row, 1972. The best single short statement on mythic structuralism.

Malinowski, Bronislaw. "Myth in Primitive Psychology." In *Magic, Science and Religion*, pp. 93-148. New York: Doubleday Anchor,

1954. While not denying the psychological dimensions of myth, Malinowski argues for a sociological-functional understanding of myths as "warrents" for social mores and norms.

Middleton, John, ed. *Myth and Cosmos*. New York: Natural History Press, 1967. A collection of essays that examine myths in various ritual and cultural contexts.

Sebeok, Thomas A., ed. *Myth: A Symposium*. Bloomington: American Folklore Society, 1958. A collection of essays ranging over a variety of myth topics from the nature of solar-myth theories to those that link myth and ritual.

Shinn, Larry. "Theories of Myth." In *Abingdon Dictionary of Living Religions*, ed. by Keith Crim. Nashville: Abingdon Press, 1981. A division of myth theories into two basic functional groups: psychological and social.

Slater, Peter. *The Dynamics of Religion*. New York: Harper & Row, 1978. Describes the role of stories in religions and how new stories help bring about change.

Turner, Victor. "Myth and Symbol." In *International Encyclopedia of the Social Sciences* 10:576-82. 1968. An appreciation of the various uses and messages symbols and myths can convey, especially related to social values and institutions.

II. Resources for the Study of Hindu Myths and Folktales

Anthologies

Basu, B. D., ed. *The Sacred Books of the Hindus*. Allahabad: Sudhindranātha Vasu, 1909-37. Primary Hindu texts in translation.

Coomaraswamy, A. K., and Sister Nivedita. *Myths of the Hindus and Buddhists*. New York: Dover Publications, 1967. An old (first published in 1913) but still useful collection of Hindu and Buddhist stories.

Kirk, James A. *Stories of the Hindus: An Introduction Through Texts and Interpretations*. New York: Macmillan, 1972. An anthology of Hindu myths from a wide historical period.

Müller, F. Max, ed. *Sacred Books of the East*. 50 vols. New Delhi: Motilal Banarsidass, 1959ff (reprint). Translations of many basic Indian religious texts.

O'Flaherty, Wendy Doniger. *Hindu Myths*. Baltimore: Penquin

Books, 1975. A translation of selected Vedic, Epic, and Puranic myths.

van Buitenen, J. A. B. *Tales of Ancient India.* Chicago: University of Chicago Press, 1959. An anthology of tales ranging from King Vikram and the goblin to Buddhist *Jataka* or birth tales.

Walker, Benjamin. *The Hindu World.* 2 vols. New York: Frederick A. Praeger, 1968. A generally reliable reference for Hindu characters, literature, etc.

Zimmer, Heinrich. *Myths and Symbols in Indian Art and Civilization,* ed. by Joseph Campbell. New York: Bollingen Foundation, 1946. A retelling and analysis of some classic Hindu myths from an art history point of view.

Fables, Folktales, and Others

Bühler, George, trans. *Laws of Manu.* Vol. 25 of *Sacred Books of the East,* ed. by F. Max Müller. New Delhi: Motilal Banarsidass, 1959ff (reprint). The most widely known of the classical texts on dharma or duty.

Dimock, Edward, trans. *The Thief of Love: Bengali Tales from Court and Village.* Chicago: University of Chicago Press, 1963. An excellent translation of a major portion of a Bengali goddess (Manasa) myth and of other folktales from Bengal.

Edgerton, Franklin. *Pañchatantra.* New Haven: American Oriental Society, 1924. A very readable translation of this famous Indian fable collection.

Emeneau, Murry Barnson. *Vetālapañcaviṅśati.* New Haven: American Oriental Society, 1934. A critically edited translation of Jambhaladatta's version of King Vikram and the goblin (*vetala*) tales.

Miller, Barbara Stoller, ed. and trans. *Love Song of the Dark Lord: Jayadeva's Gītagovinda.* New York: Columbia University Press, 1977. An excellent translation of this medieval love story of Radha and Krishna composed in verse.

Epics

Edgerton, Franklin. *The Bhagavad Gītā.* New York: Harper Torchbooks, 1964. An accurate though sometimes awkward English translation of this classic episode from the *Mahabharata.*

Ganguli, Kisari Mohan, trans. *The Mahabharata.* 12 vols. 2nd ed. Calcutta: Oriental Publishing Co., 1963. An old but complete English translation of this Hindu epic.

Griffith, Ralph T. H. *The Rámáyan of Válmíki*. 5 vols. Banaras: E. J. Lazarus, 1895. An old and dated translation which is still used because of its completeness.

Hill, Douglass P., trans. *The Holy Lake of the Acts of Rāma: Translation of Tulasī Dās's Rāmacaritamānasa*. London: Oxford University Press, 1952. An English rendering of the shorter Hindi version of the *Ramayana* including an altered ending to this famous tale.

Narasimhan, Chakravarthi V. *The Mahābhārata: An English Version Based on Selected Verses*. New Delhi: Oxford Book Company, 1965. A clear translation of the main story line (battle between Kauravas and Pandavas) of this huge Indian epic.

van Buitenen, J. A. B. *The Book of the Beginning*. Chicago: University of Chicago Press, 1974ff. An excellent translation of and introduction to the *Mahabharata*, which remains unfinished due to the untimely death of the author.

Williams, Sir. M. M. *Indian Epic Poetry*. London: Williams & Norgate, 1963. An outline of the basic stories of the *Ramayana* and *Mahabharata*.

Zaehner, Robert C. *The Bhagavad-Gītā*. London: Oxford University Press, 1969. Includes both the Sanskrit text and a very readable English translation of this Indian classic.

Puranas

Bhaktivedanta, A. C. Swami. *Śrīmad-Bhāgavatam*. 30 vols. completed. Los Angeles: Bhaktivedanta Book Trust, 1972ff. Sanskrit text, Roman transliteration, English translation, and commentary form the format of this valuable work. The tenth canto comprising the life of Krishna is unfinished due to the author's death.

Dimmitt, Cornelia, and J. A. B. van Buitenen, eds. and trans. *Classical Hindu Mythology: A Reader in the Sanskrit Purānas*. Philadelphia: Temple University Press, 1978. A wide-ranging and skillful selection and translation of major Puranic (devotional, theistic) mythology.

Śiva Purāṇa. Ancient Indian Tradition and Mythology, vols. 1-4. New Delhi: Motilal Banarsidass, 1970. One of the eighteen major *Puranas*, or "Legend" collections, in this case devoted to the god Shiva.

Wilson, Horace Hayman. *The Vishnu Purana*. 5 vols. London: Kegan Paul, Trench, Trübner, 1864-77. An old but complete translation of this central Vishnu/Krishna story collection.

Secondary Studies

Archer, W. G. *The Loves of Krishna in Indian Painting and Poetry.*
London: George Allen & Unwin, 1957. Provides examples of the
iconographic and literary uses made of Krishna stories.

Bhattacharji, Sukumari. *The Indian Theogony.* Cambridge: Cambridge University Press, 1972. An explication of Indian (Hindu)
mythology from a comparative and structural point of view.

Dumont, Louis. "A Structural Definition of a Folk Deity of Tamil
Nad: Aiyanar, the Lord." In *Reader in Comparative Religion,*
ed. by William A. Lessa and Evon Z. Vogt, pp. 189-195. 3rd ed.
New York: Harper & Row, 1972. A structural study of the myth
and cult of a South Indian village deity.

Hiltebeitel, Alf. *The Ritual of Battle: Krishna in the Mahabharata.*
Ithaca: Cornell University Press, 1976. A superb study of selected
issues and characters that centers upon the notion of sacrifice in
this great Hindu epic.

Kinsley, David. *The Sword and the Flute.* Berkeley: University of
California Press, 1977. A sensitive study of the cults and myths
of Krishna and Kali.

O'Flaherty, Wendy Doniger. *Asceticism and Eroticism in the Mythology of Śiva.* New York: Oxford University Press, 1973. A
Lévi-Straussian analysis of Shiva mythology of unusually high
quality.

—————. *The Origins of Evil in Hindu Mythology.* Berkeley: University of California Press, 1976. An interesting study of selected Indian myths approached from several disciplinary vantage points.

III. Resource for the Study of Buddhist Stories

Anthologies

Coomaraswamy, Ananda K. *Buddha and the Gospel of Buddhism.*
New York: Harper & Row, 1964. An introduction to Buddhism,
including stories about Buddha's life.

de Bary, William Theodore, ed. *The Buddhist Tradition in India,
China and Japan.* Helpful translations of various scriptures and
stories.

Piyadassi Thera. *Stories of Buddhist India.* Vol. 1. 2nd rev. ed. Co-
lombo: Sri Lanka Bauddha Samitiya, 1953. A very helpful re-
source.

Stryk, Lucien, ed. *World of the Buddha: A Reader—from the Three Baskets to Modern Zen*. New York: Doubleday & Co., 1968. Primary texts in translation.

Warren, Henry Clarke. *Buddhism in Translation*. New York: Atheneum, 1963. A selection of somewhat dated translations.

Woodward, F. L. *Some Sayings of the Buddha According to the Pali Canon*. London: Oxford University Press, 1973. A representative selection of Theravada texts.

Stories

Burlingame, E. W., trans. *Buddhist Parables*. New Haven: Yale University Press, 1922. English translations of stories told by Pali commentators.

Cowell, E. B., ed. *The Jātaka, or Stories of the Buddha's Former Births*. London: Pali Text Society, 1973. All 547 Pali *Jatakas* in English translation.

Rhys Davids, Mrs. C. A. F., ed. *Buddhist Birth Stories*. London: Routledge and Kegan Paul, 1925. Selected *Jatakas*, and the *Introduction to the Jatakas*, the earliest Pali language biography of the Buddha.

———. *The Minor Anthologies of the Pali Canon, Part IV*. Trans. by Jean Kennedy and Henry S. Gehman. London: Pali Text Society, 1974. Contains "Vimānavatthu: Stories of the Mansions" and "Petavatthu: Stories of the Departed."

Speyer, Jacob Samuel. *The Jatakamālā, or Garland of Birth-Stories, by Arya Sūra*. London: Henry Frowde, 1895. A Mahayana collection of *Jatakas*.

Stories of Old, Gathered from the Pali Commentaries. Wheel Publication no. 59. Kandy: Buddhist Publication Society, 1963. Narratives about early monks.

Biographies of the Buddha

Arnold, Sir Edwin. *The Light of Asia*. New York: Doubleday, 1894, and many reprints. A poetic, free translation of the *Lalitavistara;* very influential on Western writers.

Jones, J. J., trans. *The Mahāvastu*. 3 vols. London: Luzac & Co., 1949. A long Sanskrit biography of Buddha in translation.

Last Days of the Buddha. Wheel Publication nos. 67-69. Kandy: Buddhist Publication Society, 1964. Complete translation of the *Mahaparinibbana Sutta* about the final events of Buddha's life.

Ñānamoli, Bhikkhu. *The Life of the Buddha.* Kandy: Buddhist Publication Society, 1972. A biography composed mainly of selections from the Pali canon.

Saddhatissa, H. *The Life of the Buddha.* London: George Allen & Unwin, 1976. A brief retelling for modern, Western readers.

Secondary Studies

Amore, Roy C. *Two Masters, One Message.* Nashville: Abingdon Press, 1978. Includes a comparison of stories told about Buddha and Christ.

Horner, I. B. *Women Under Primitive Buddhism.* London: Routledge and Sons, 1930. A study of the place and role of women in India before and after the Buddha.

Thomas, E. J. *The Life of Buddha As Legend and History.* London: Kegan Paul, Trench, Trübner, 1952 (orig. pub. 1927). A critical study of the various stories told about the Buddha.

Winternitz, Maurice. *Buddhist Literature and Jaina Literature.* Vol. 2 of *A History of Indian Literature.* Calcutta: University of Calcutta, 1938. A scholarly survey of the various Buddhist texts.